KIDS CALLIGRAPHY

A BEGINNER'S GUIDE TO BRUSH PEN CALLIGRAPHY

EMMA PEARCE-HAGEN

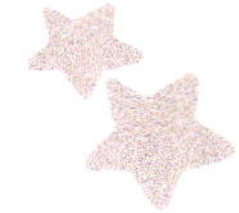

Kids Calligraphy

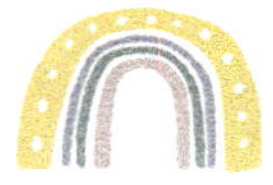

First printing, 2023
ISBN: 978-1-7386162-2-0 (Paperback)

Inkberry Press
Auckland, New Zealand

Cover by Emma Pearce-Hagen
Calligraphy and Illustrations: Emma Pearce-Hagen
Photos: John Hagen
Photo Model: Isla Hosking
Author photo: Haley Adele Photography

Visit the author's website at www.inkberry.co.nz

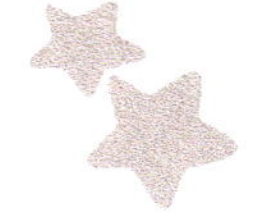

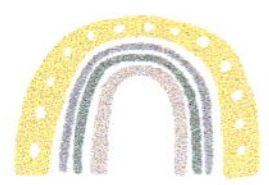

Kids Calligraphy

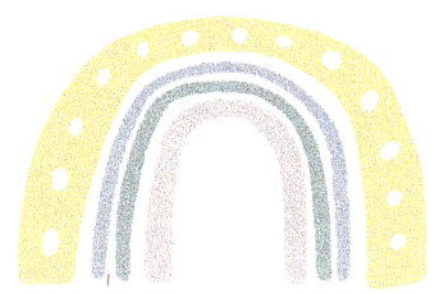

Kids Calligraphy CONTENTS

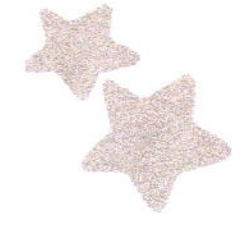

Kids Calligraphy

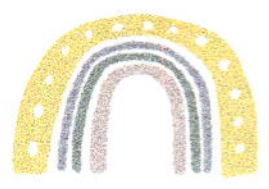

WELCOME to the Kids Calligraphy Guide to Modern Brush Pen Calligraphy!

Do you what the word 'Calligraphy' means? The word comes from the Greek language. 'Kallos' meaning beauty and 'graphein' meaning 'write'. So 'calligraphy' means beautiful writing. In this book we are going to learn the art of beautiful writing.
Brush pen calligraphy is such a fun hobby. It's not only fun though! Calligraphy will also be useful in lots of art projects. Bookmarks, wall art and greeting cards are just some of the cool projects you can use with calligraphy.

Did you know calligraphy has lots of other benefits too? Learning to write calligraphy encourages creativity and is a practical skill you can use all your life. Having beautiful handwriting is becoming a lost art because many children are using a keyboard more often. Calligraphy is also good for your brain! Writing by hand helps you remember important information. It also helps develop fine motor skills and coordination. That means you are better at doing delicate tasks with your fingers. Calligraphy takes a lot of patience and practice to learn so you will become resilient. It will also develop concentration and mindfulness. How cool is that?! In a fast paced, digital world I believe it's really important for you to slow down, focus and work with your hands.

Just work your way through each page and follow the instructions. There are plenty of opportunities to practice your new skills as you go along. You can write directly on the book pages or you can put some paper over the pages when you write. Don't get frustrated and give up! Enjoy the process of learning and the journey of calligraphy.

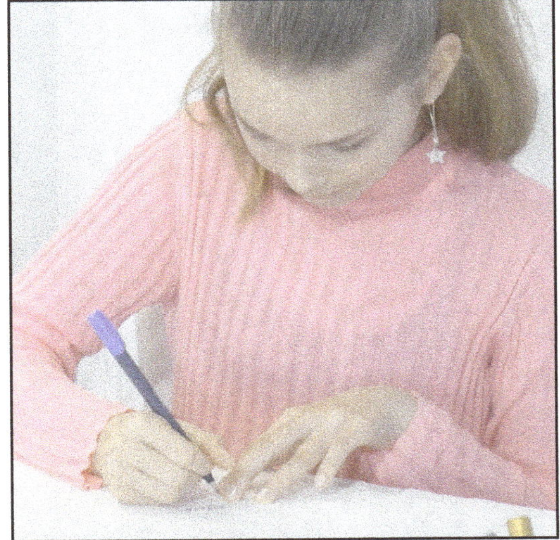
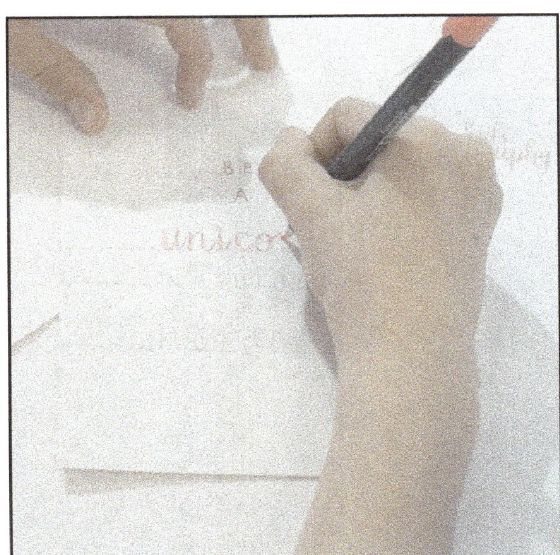
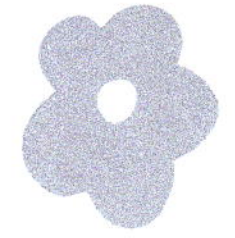

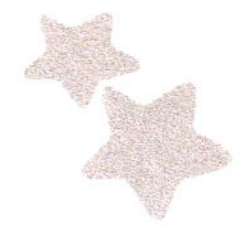

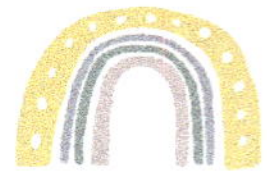

Before you start learning to write calligraphy,
you will need a few supplies from the list below.

Brush Calligraphy Pens

There are lots of different brush calligraphy pens to choose from but my favourites are called Tombow Fudenosuke. They have a firm tip but are flexible. That means they are easy to use. You can choose from lots of colours too! You can get Tombow pens from most Art Supplies stores. Which is your favourite colour?

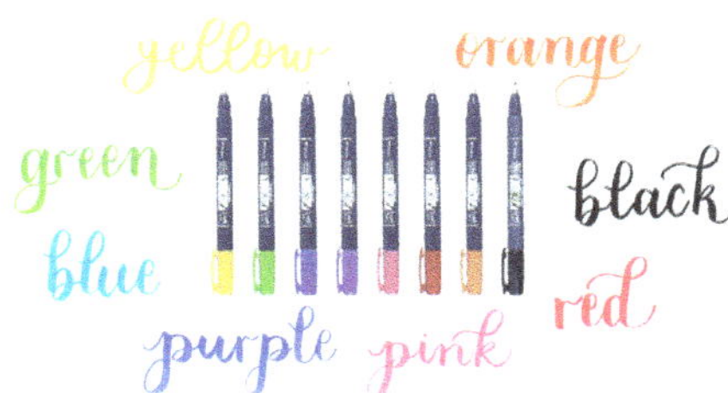

Paper

When you are learning Brush Pen Calligraphy, it's a good idea to use a see-through paper to practice your lettering. That way you can put the paper over the worksheets to practice if you don't want to write in your book. Make sure you choose paper that is smooth. Good papers to use are called Zeta paper or HP premium paper. When you get more confident you can choose paper and card in lots of different colours to make bookmarks, greeting cards or wall art.

Craft Supplies

You can use your brush calligraphy writing for lots of fun projects! It's handy to have some extra supplies to help you create colourful art works.
These are some supplies that you can get from most stationery stores:

Pencil and ruler	Coloured card
Scissors	Patterned paper
Glue	Gold leaf or glitter
Hole Punch	Ribbons and tassles

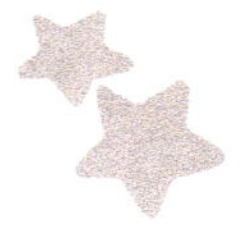

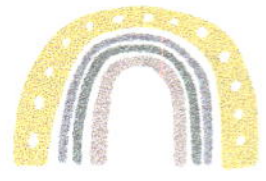

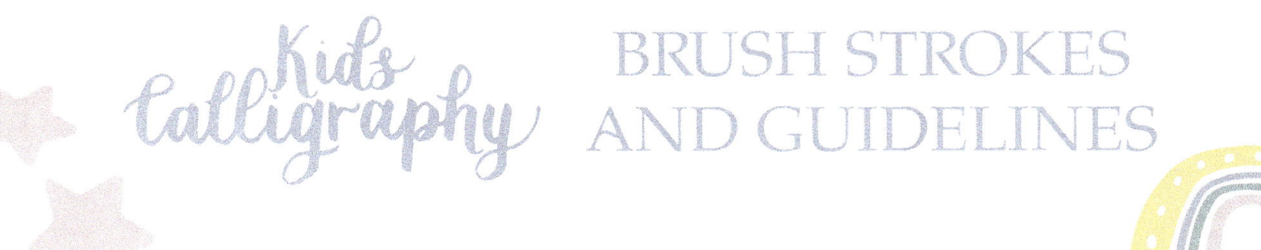

Remember when we chatted about calligraphy and how that word means beautiful writing?

The way we make our writing beautiful is to keep our letter strokes on the same angle, and the letters at the same height. So, when you start learning calligraphy, it's a good idea to use guidelines to practice. You can use the guidelines in the worksheet section and there are some extra practice pages at the back of the book.

Try to keep all your alphabet letters on the base line. The lower case letters a, c, e, i, m, n, o, r, s, u, v, w, and x fit in the x-height. The x-height shows you how big these letters should be.

The lower case letters b, d, f, h, k, l, and t have an ascender and go from the base line to the top line. The lower case letters g, j, p, q, and y have a descender and go to the bottom line. The capital letters go from the base line to the top line.

 The guidelines help keep your letters straight up and down.

When you start using your brush pen, you need to learn how to make thick and thin strokes. To make a thick stroke, just push your pen a bit harder when you move your pen down. You just need a little bit of pressure. When you do a thin stroke on the upstroke , you don't use any pressure. Make the stroke nice and light.

REMEMBER THIS !
Use a thick stroke on a letter downstroke
Use a thin stroke on a letter upstroke

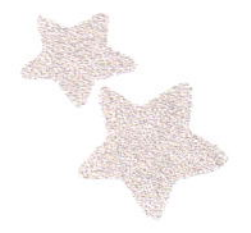

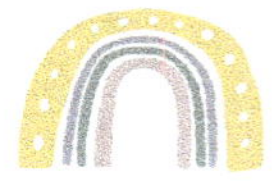

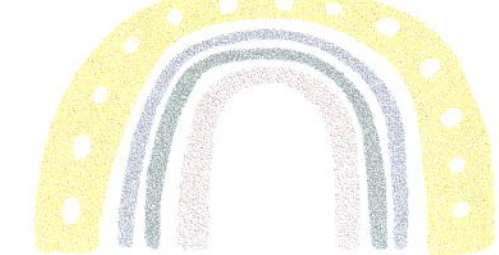

Do you remember that when you start using your brush pen, you need to use thick and thin strokes? To make a thick stroke, just push your pen a bit harder when you move your pen down. You just need a little bit of pressure. When you do a thin stroke on the upstroke, you don't use any pressure.

But to do that, you need to hold your pen properly. Grip the pen comfortably with your thumb and first finger at the bottom of the pen near the nib. Just like a normal pen or pencil! You also need to make sure that the paper, your hand, and the pen are on a 45 degree angle. That is so you can apply the correct pressure on the strokes. If your hand and pen are parallel to the page, you won't be able to do a thick downstroke.

It's very important that your strokes are nice and smooth, so don't push on the nib of the pen too hard. Also, if you push the pen too hard the nib of the pen will fray.

Go slow and keep practicing holding you pen on the correct angle and doing the thick and thin strokes.

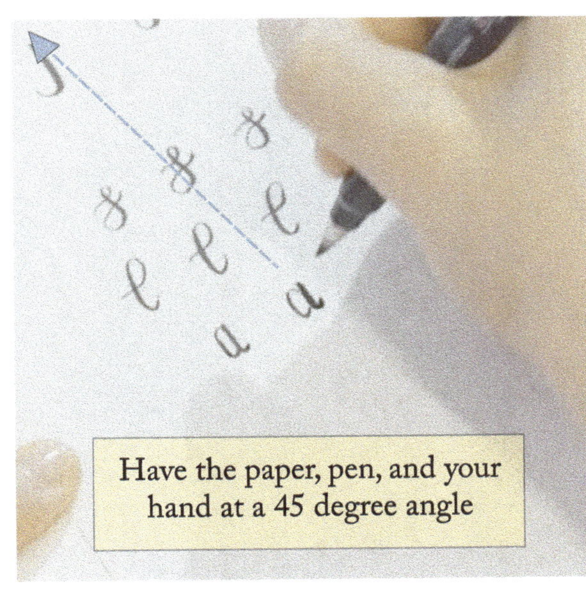

Have the paper, pen, and your
hand at a 45 degree angle

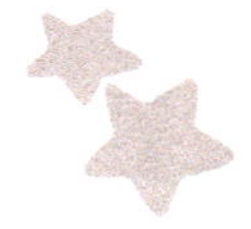
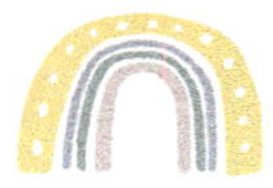

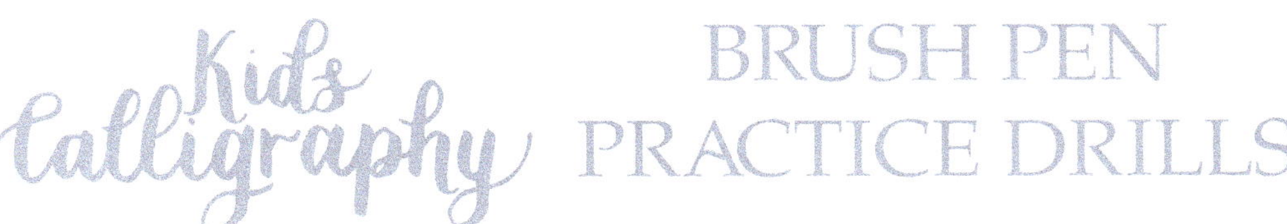

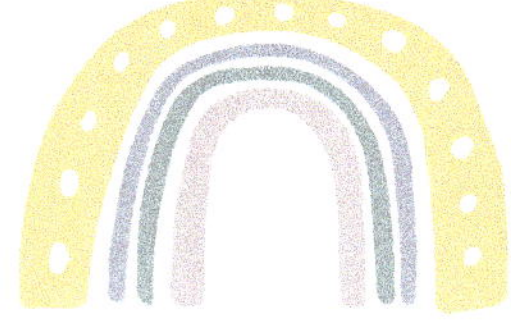

Now it's your turn to practice using your brush pen. Move your paper to a 45 degree angle and hold your pen at a 45 degree angle too. Try doing some thick down strokes by pushing your pen a bit harder when you move your pen down. Then you can try doing some thin upstrokes. Remember to make the upstroke nice and light. Practice using the guidelines to do your strokes straight up and down.
Have fun!

THICK DOWNSTROKE   GUIDELINES

X-HEIGHT
BASE
LINE

THIN UPSTROKE   GUIDELINES

X-HEIGHT
BASE
LINE

REMEMBER THIS!
Use a thick stroke on a letter downstroke
Use a thin stroke on a letter upstroke

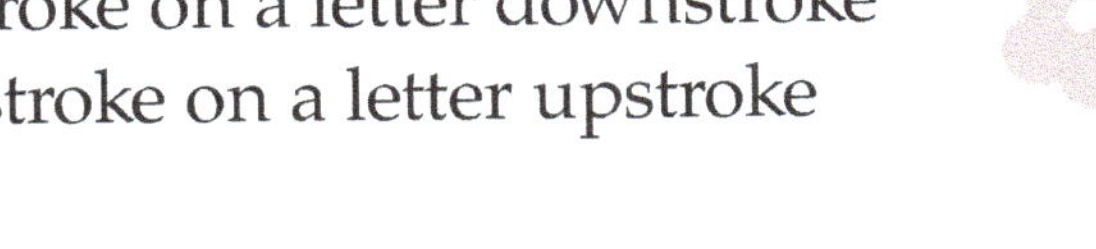

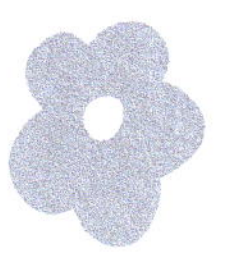

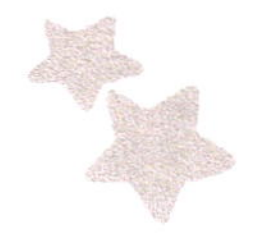
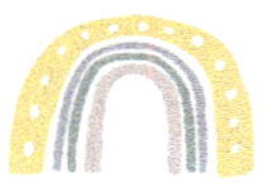

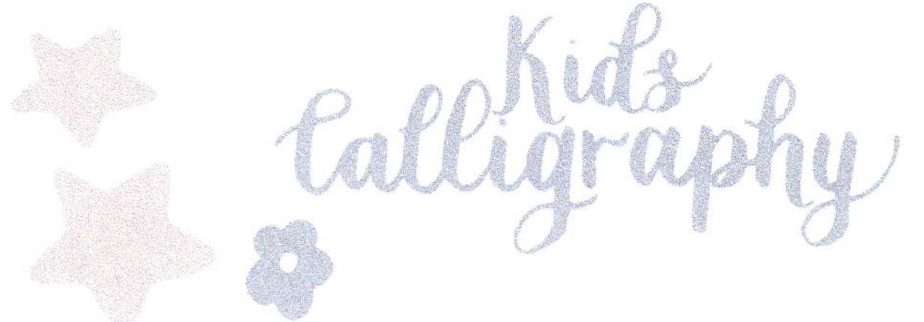 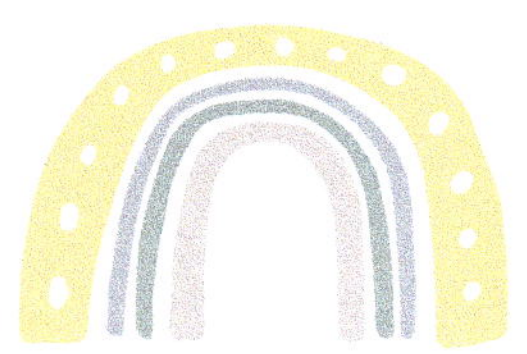

FOUNDATION STROKES

Foundation strokes are the basic strokes that you can use to write a lot of letters in the lower case alphabet. If you practice the strokes, you can combine them together to make other letters.

There are six strokes that are very useful to learn. Let's have a look at the names of the different strokes.

1. The underturn stroke. This stroke helps you make the letters i, u, v, w, and y.
2. The overturn stroke. This stroke helps you make the letters h, m, and n.
3. The ascender stroke. This stroke helps you make the letters b, d, h, k, l, and t
4. The descender stroke. This stroke helps you to make the letters g, j, p, q, and y
5. The oval stroke. This stroke helps you make the letters a, c, d, e, g, and o
6. The reverse oval stroke. This stroke helps you make the letters b and p.

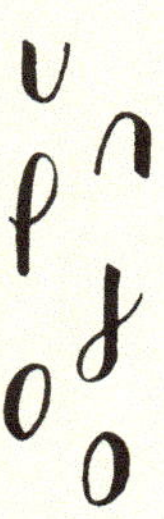

NOW IT'S YOUR TURN!!

Practice using your brush pens by following the arrows and writing the foundation strokes. Remember to put a little bit of pressure on the downstroke to make it thick and no pressure on the upstroke to make it thin. Use the guidelines to make sure your letters are straight up and down. Just try your best and have fun!!

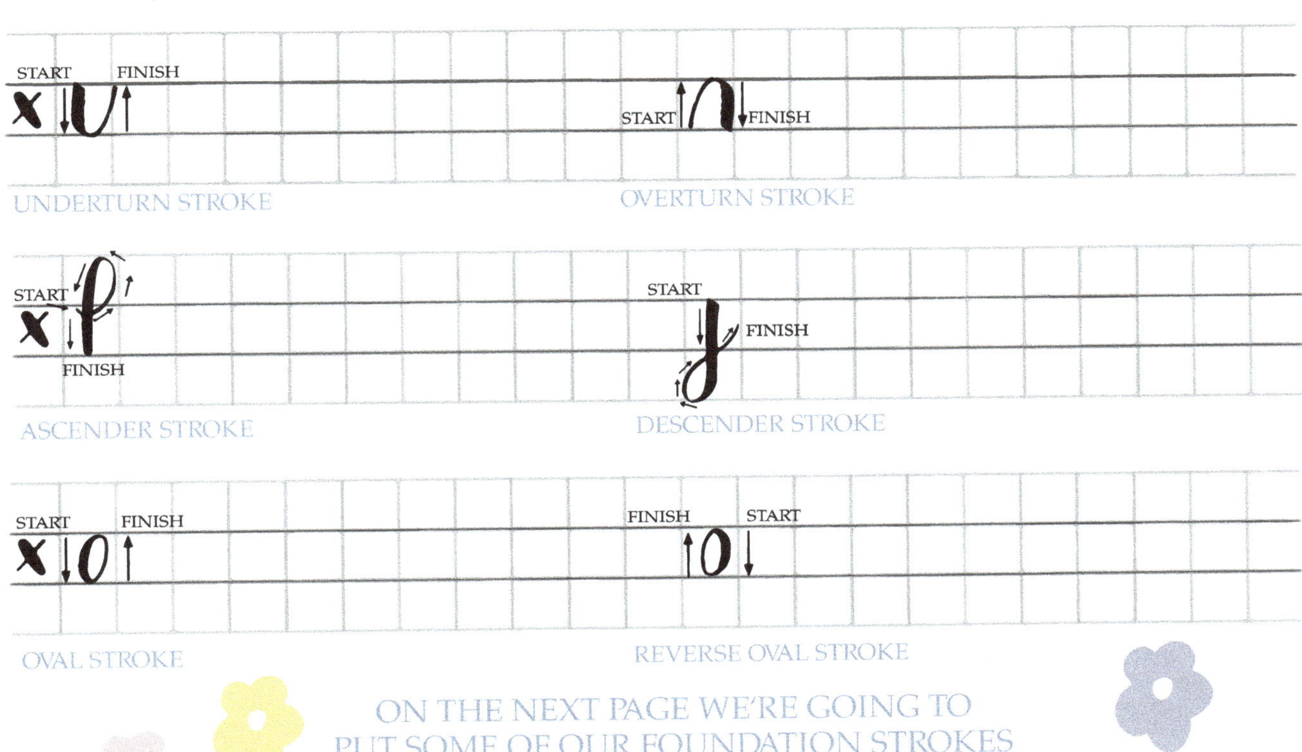

ON THE NEXT PAGE WE'RE GOING TO PUT SOME OF OUR FOUNDATION STROKES TOGETHER TO MAKE SOME LETTERS

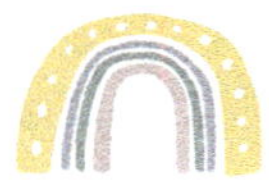

Now you have practiced the Foundation strokes, you can put the strokes together to make some of the letters in the lower case alphabet. This will help you to write the letters beautifully. You might need to add an extra stroke and you can add a little flourish at the end of some of the letters to make it look super special. Practice putting the strokes together to make the letters below.

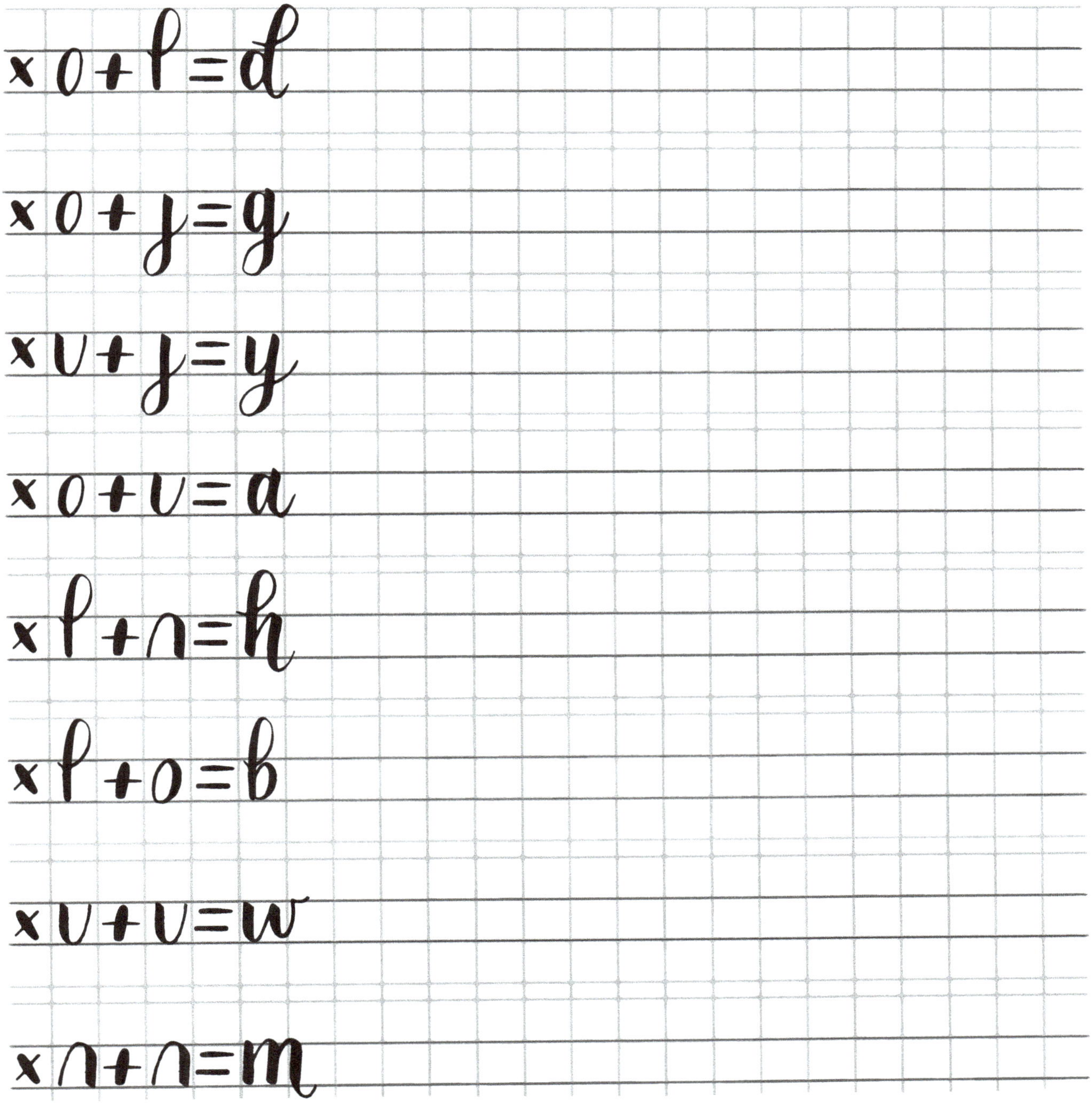

BRUSH PEN CALLIGRAPHY ALPHABET SAMPLER

UPPER CASE ALPHABET

A B C D E F G
H I J K L M N
O P Q R S T U
V W X Y Z

LOWER CASE ALPHABET

a b c d e f g
h i j k l m n
o p q r s t u
v w x y z

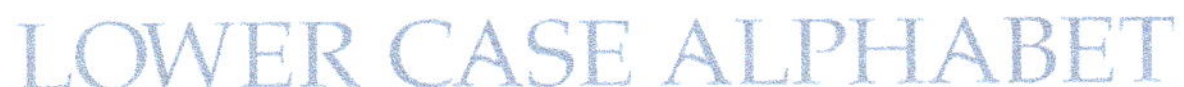
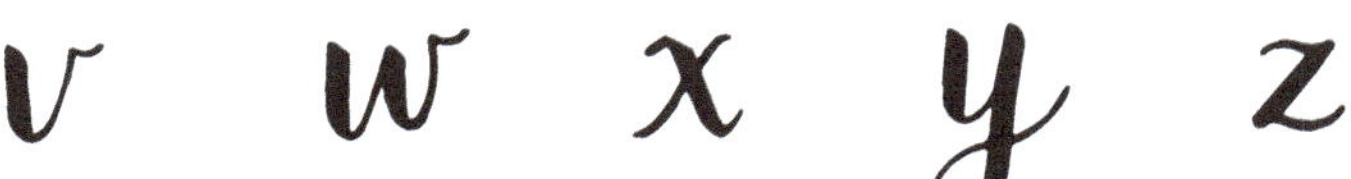
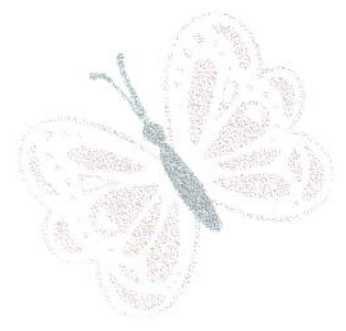

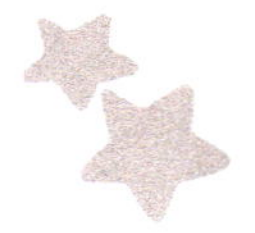
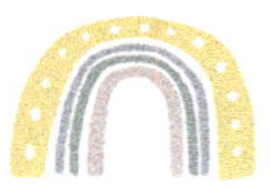

SIMPLE CAPITALS
ALPHABET SAMPLER

A B C D E F

G H I J K L M

N O P Q R S T

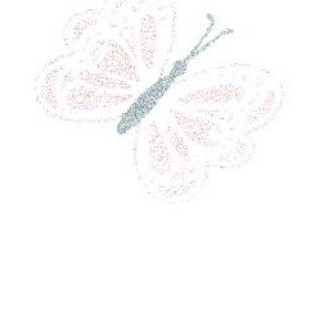

U V W X Y Z

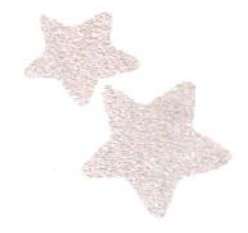

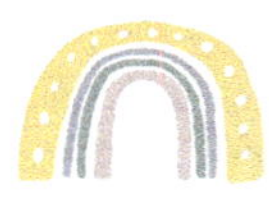

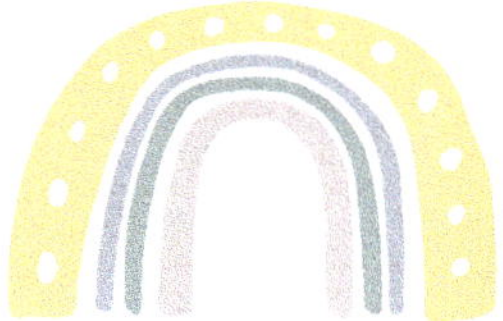

WELL DONE! YOU'RE DOING GREAT!

You've learned lots of new skills already! You can hold your pen correctly, you know how to do thick downstrokes and thin upstrokes, you've learned your foundation strokes, and put some of those strokes together to make some letters.

So, on the next pages you are going to practice all the letters of the alpahabet! Start with the Lower Case letters (small letters). On the worksheets, write each letter three or four times.

When you feel confident, move onto the next letter in the alphabet.

When you've practiced the lower case letters, you can try the Upper Case letters (capitals).

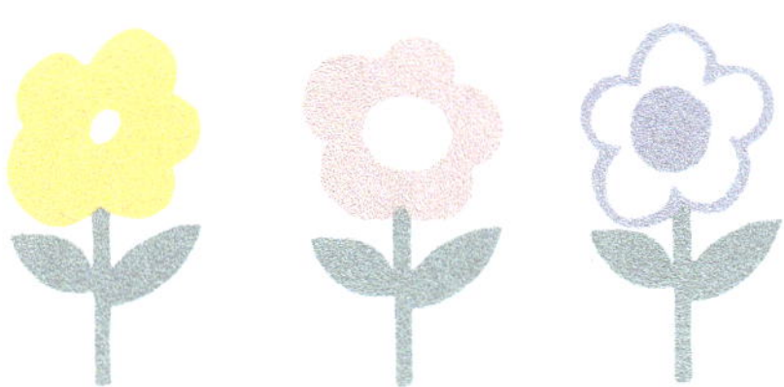

Remember when we chatted about how calligraphy takes a lot of patience and practice to learn? This is the time to become resilient. Don't give up on practicing your letters. Because when you've written all your letters, the fun begins and you can start writing words!

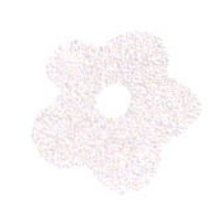

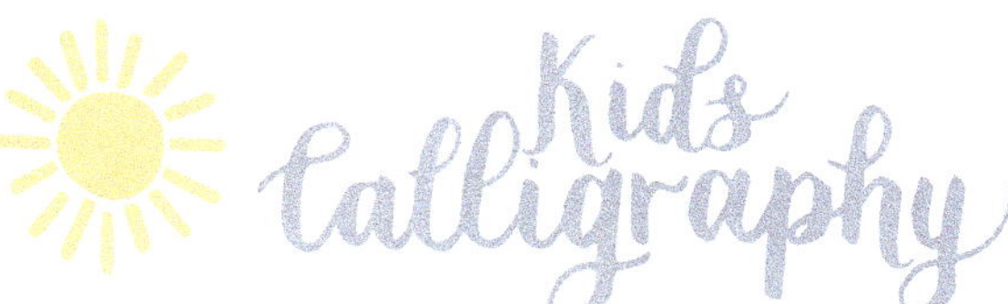

x *a* a a

x *b* b b

x *c* c c

x *d* d d

x *e* e e

x *f* f f

x *g* g g

x *h* h h

x *i* i i

x *j* j j

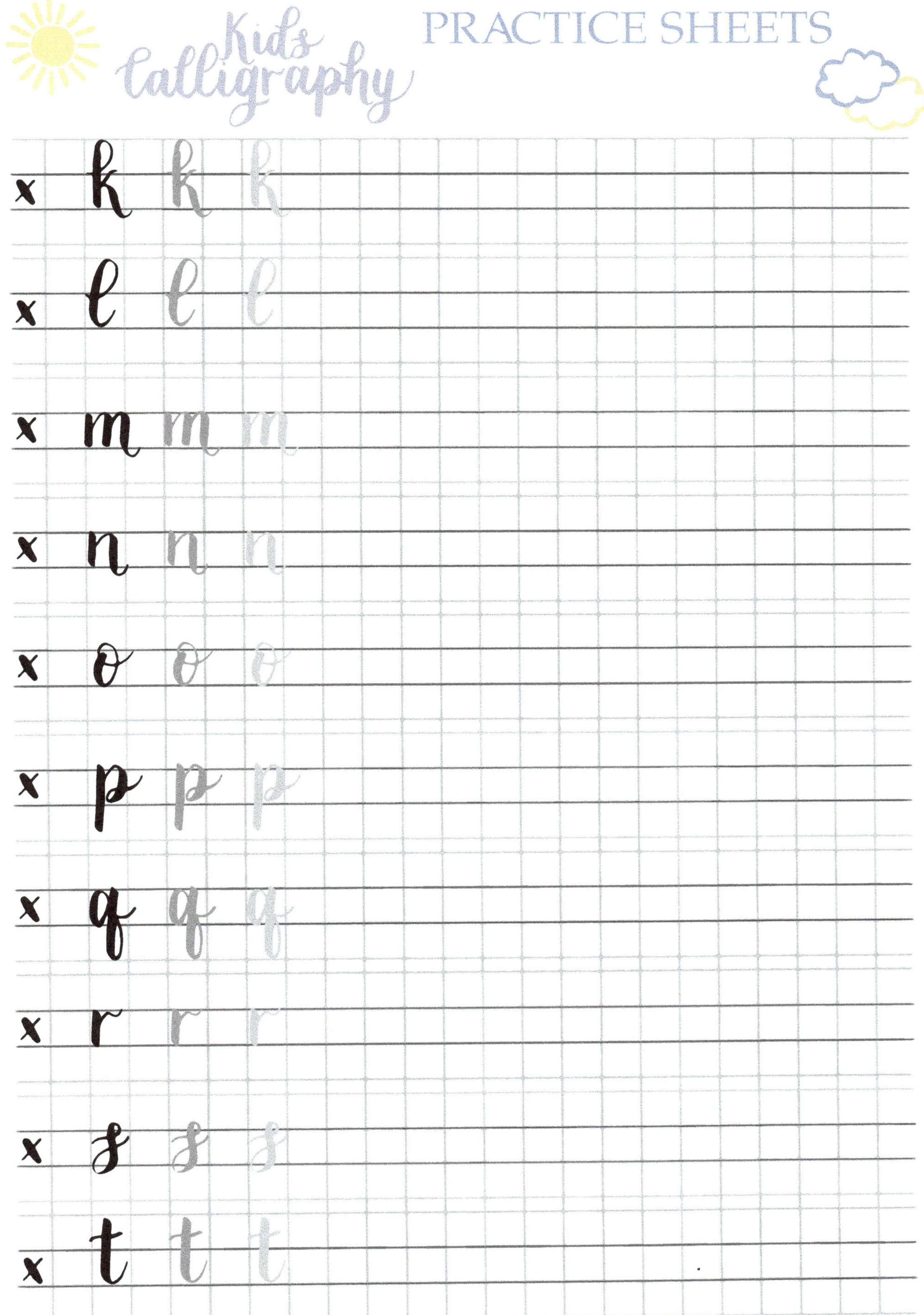

x u u u

x v v v

x w w w

x x x x

x y y y

x z z z

GREAT JOB!

Now you've practiced all your lower case letters, keep going!
Practice your upper case letters now.

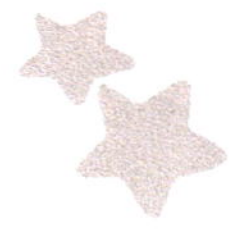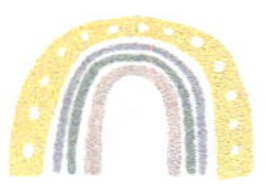

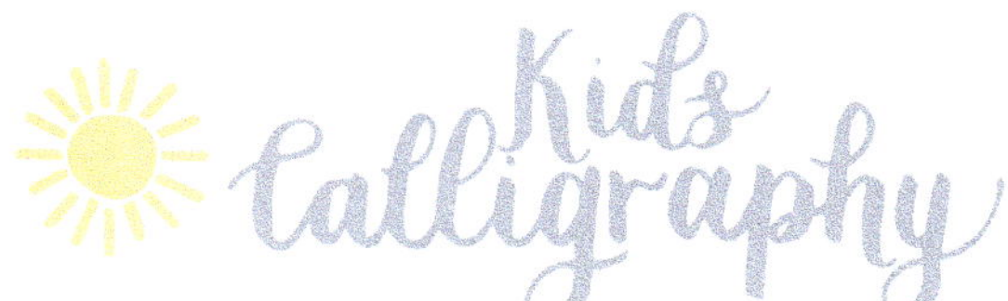

x A A A

x B B B

x C C C

x D D D

x E E E

x F F F

x G G G

x H H H

x I I I

x J J J

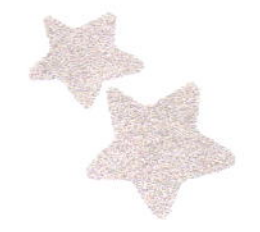

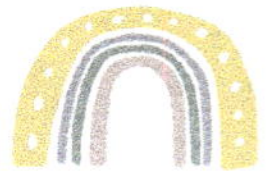

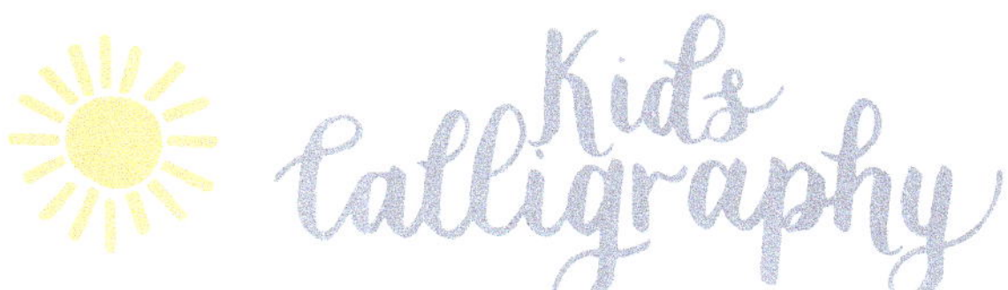

x K K K

x L L L

x m m m

x n n n

x O O O

x p p p

x Q Q Q

x R R R

x S S S

x T T T

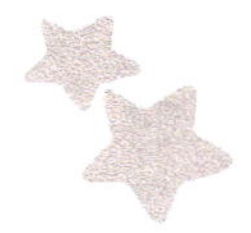

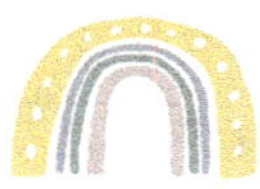

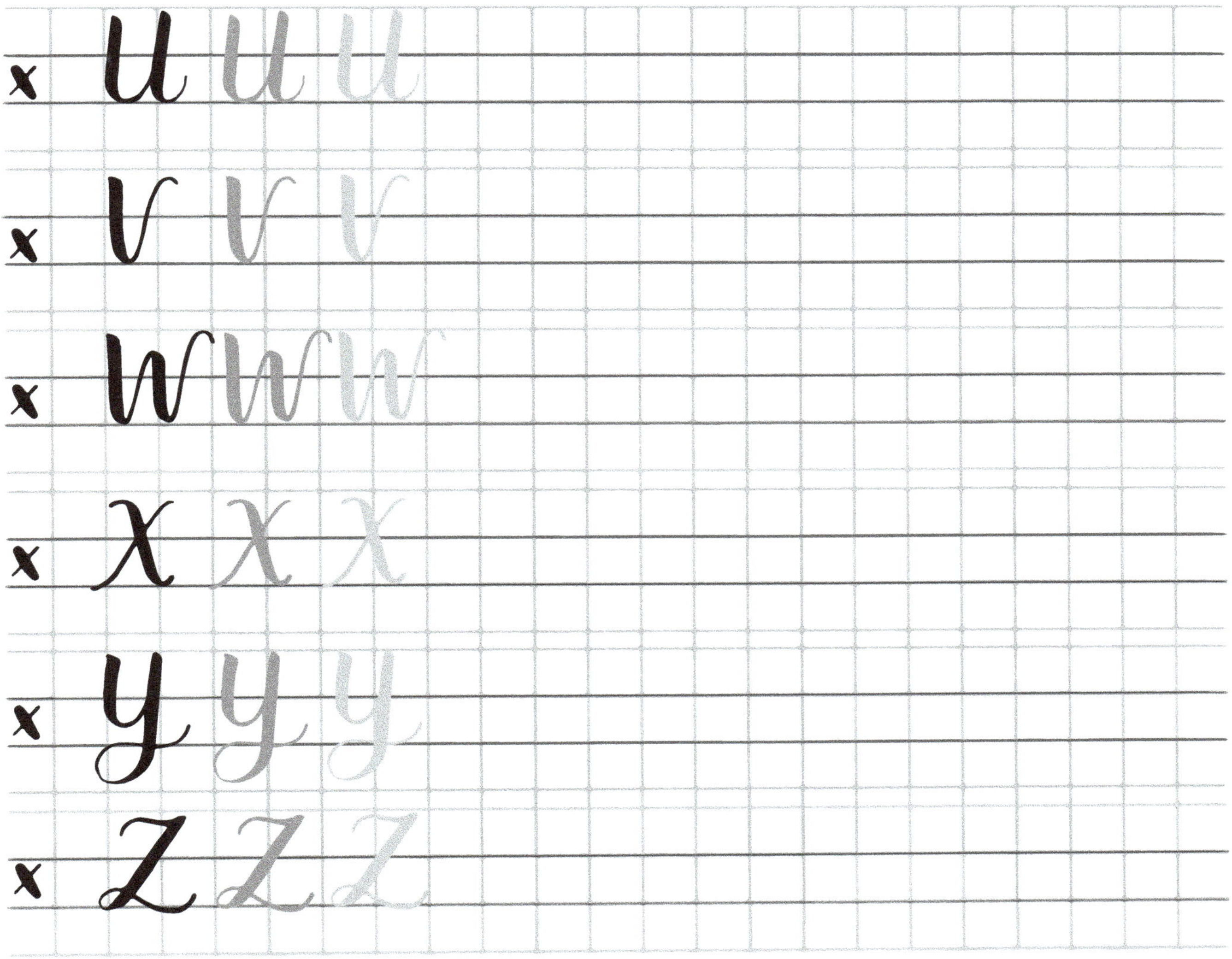

x U U U

x V V V

x W W W

x X X X

x Y Y Y

x Z Z Z

GREAT JOB!

Now that you've practiced all your brush pen calligraphy letters, keep going! Let's move on to linking our letters together to make some words.

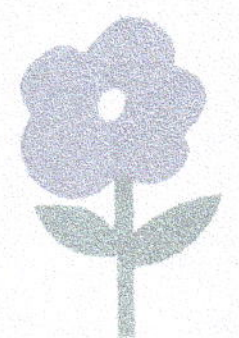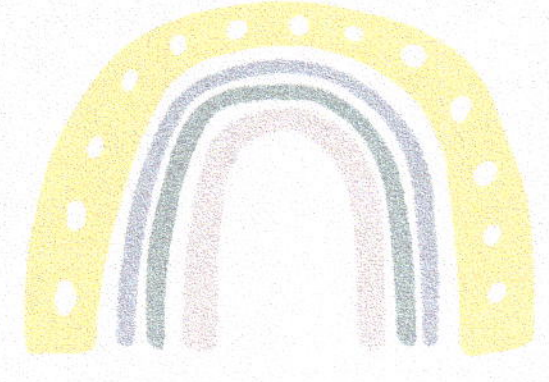

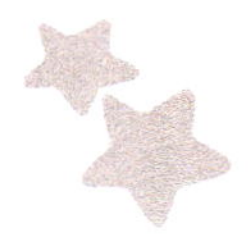

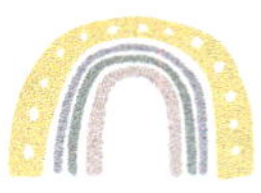

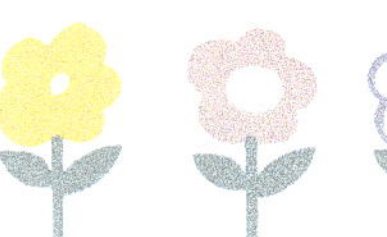

Now that you've practiced all your brush pen calligraphy letters, let's try to link the letters together to make some words.

After each letter, extend the pen stroke to link onto the next letter. If you want to, you can take off your pen between letters. You can see how the strokes of the are extended in each letter below.

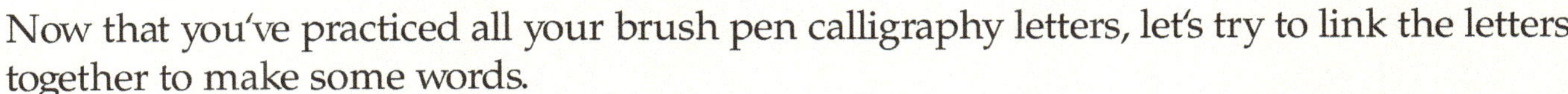

When the stroke on each letter is extended you will be able to join it onto the next letter. Remember it's okay to take the pen off and stop between the letters. You may need to take the pen off to start the stroke of the next letter sometimes too. For example, with the 'k' you start the letter on the bottom of the loop.

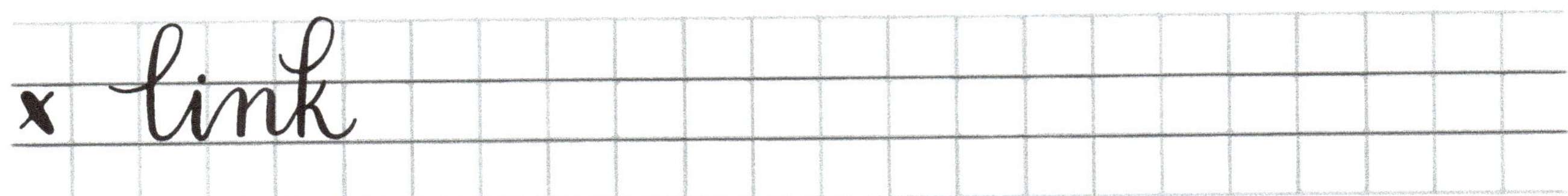

NOW IT'S YOUR TURN!

Try to write the word 'link' on the lines below. Remember to use light pressure on the upstroke and heavier pressure on the downstroke.

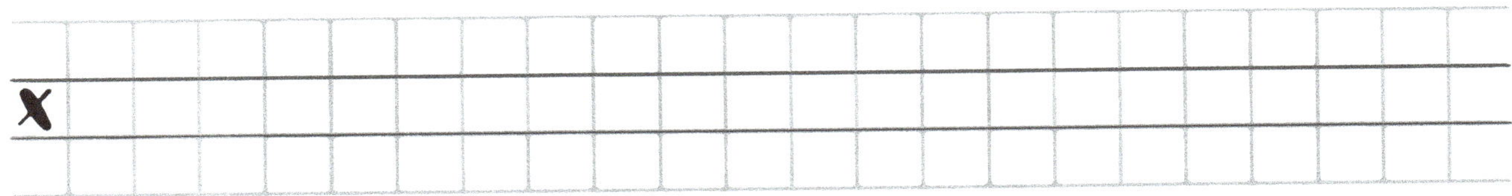

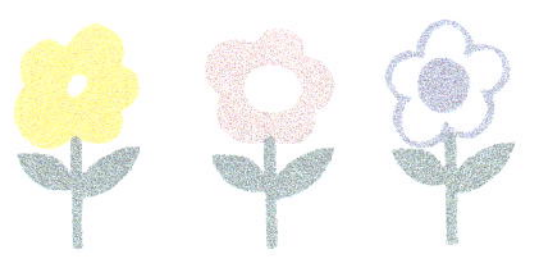

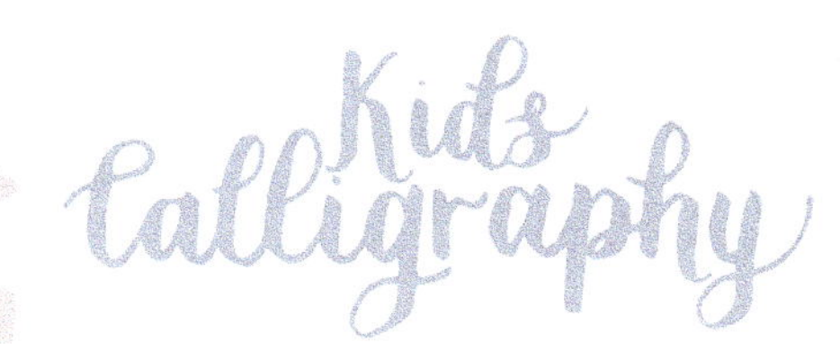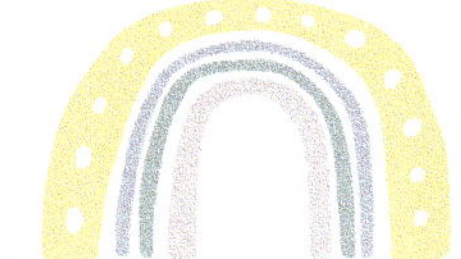

The first word we are going to write with brush pen calligraphy is your name!
I'll show you the steps with my name "Emma".

1. I'm going to practice the letters in my name; a capital 'E', a lower case 'm' and a lower case 'a'. I found the letters on the worksheet practice sheets.

2. I'm going to write each letter about 8 times. I'll use the grid and the x height so I can make sure that my letters were straight up and down and at the correct height.

3. Now, I'm going to join up all the letters to write my name. Can you see how I have linked the letters to each other?

4. It's your turn now! Find the letters of your name in the sampler or practice sheets and then write each letter on the next practice page. Write the letters a few times. When you are ready, join the letters together to make your name. Have fun!!

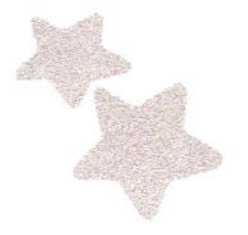
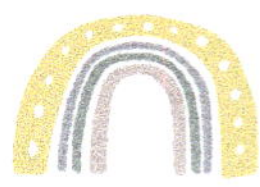

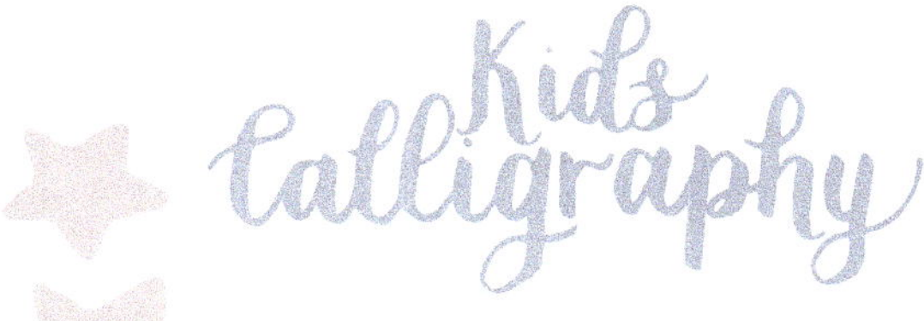

INSTRUCTIONS

It's your turn now! Find the letters of your name in the sampler or practice sheets and then write each letter a few times. When you are ready, join the letters together to make your name. Have fun!!

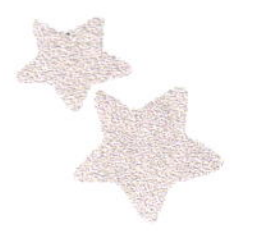
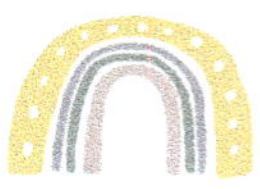

WRITING YOUR NAME PRACTICE

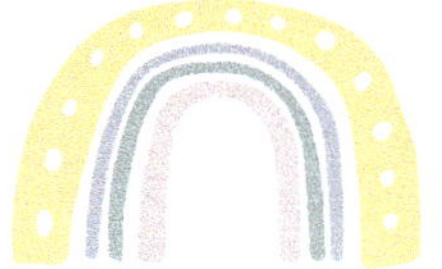

EXTRA PRACTICE SPACE IN CASE
YOU HAVE A LONG NAME!

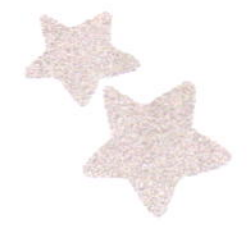

Kids
Calligraphy

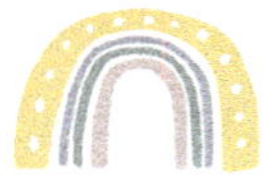

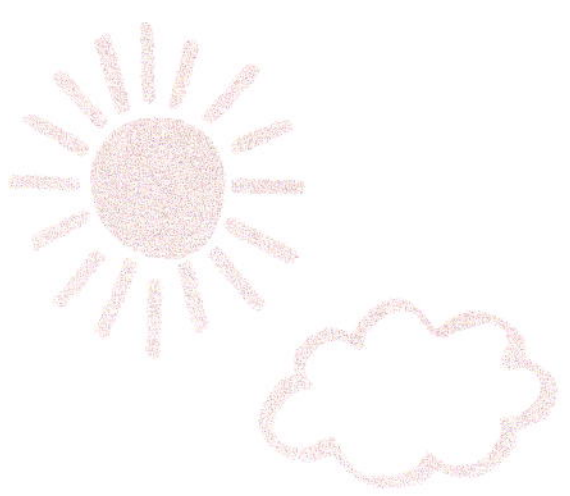

Who doesn't love to flourish?
It just makes everything more fancy, decorative, and magical. Flourishes range from a simple curve to multiple loops. You can actually follow your creativity with flourishing, but there are definitely some ways to add flourishes that will make your letters and words more beautiful.

Where can you add flourishes?
Look at the example below. Flourishes have been added at the start of the word, an upper loop on a ascender letter, a lower loop on a descender letter, and at the end of a word.
You don't have to add loops in all of these areas so just choose what you think looks best.

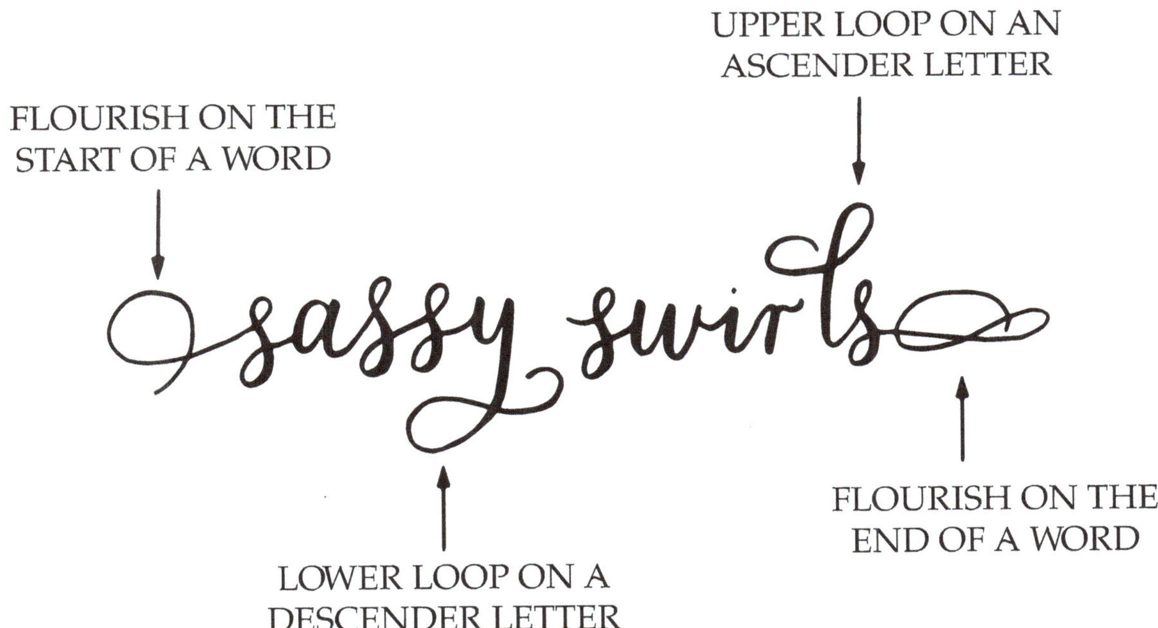

NOW ITS YOUR TURN!
On the next page, practice doing some flourishes with your brush pen.
Follow the arrows to make the flourishes.

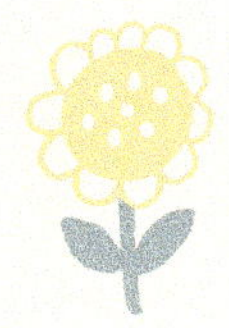

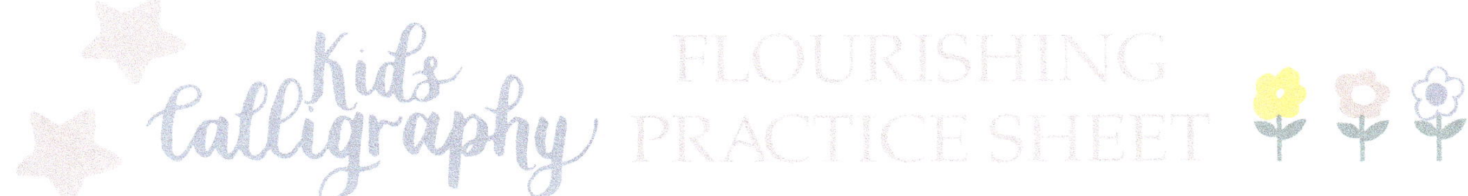

NOW ITS YOUR TURN!

Here are some different flourishing strokes. Practice doing some flourishes with your brush pen underneath the examples. You don't need to put much pressure on your brush pen. Follow the arrows to make the flourishes.

START OF A WORD

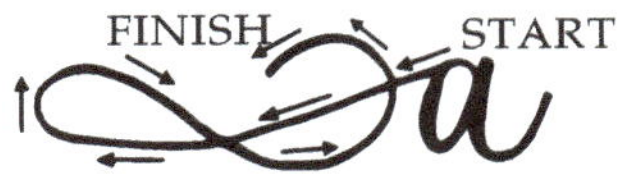

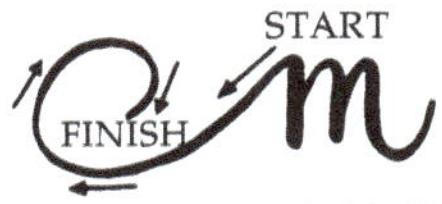

UPPER LOOP ON AN ASCENDER

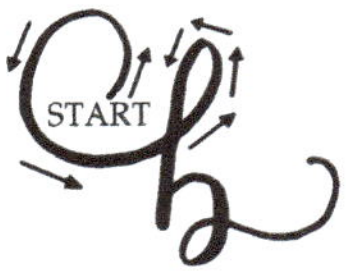

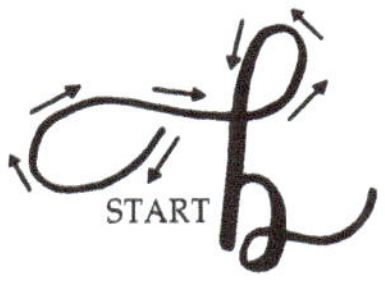

LOWER LOOP ON A DESCENDER

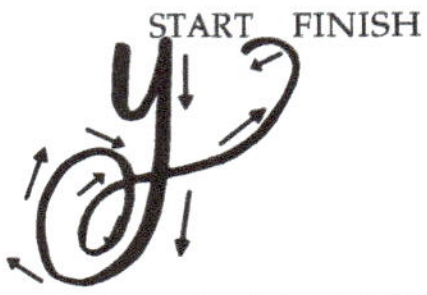

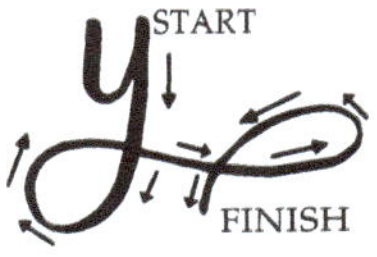

END OF A WORD

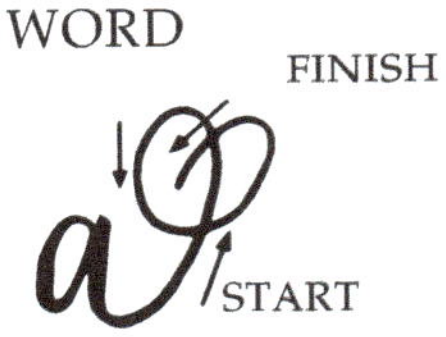

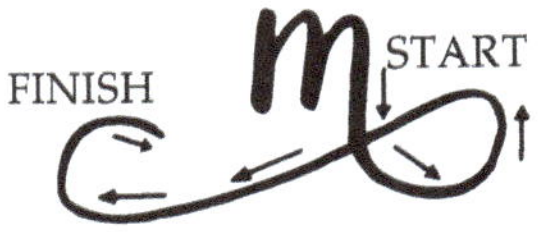

BRUSH PEN CALLIGRAPHY

PROJECTS

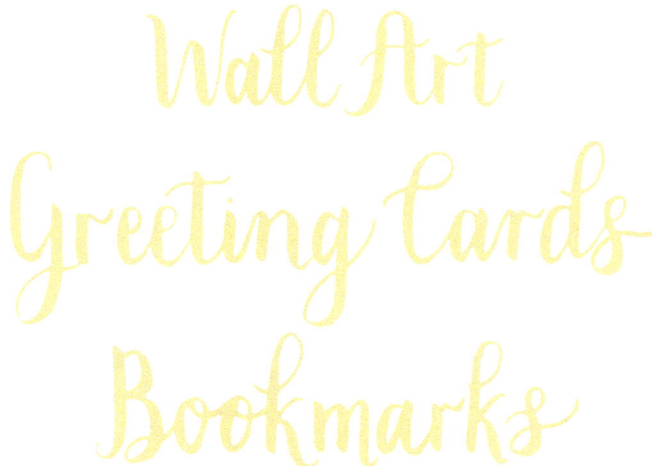

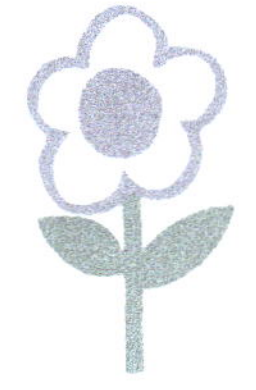

Using your Brush Pen Calligraphy to make Wall Art is lots of fun!
You can choose your own special quotes to letter, decorate and frame.
Decorate your room with positive sayings so you can see them everyday. To practice your lettering you can copy and decorate the wall art quotes on the next few pages.

SUPPLIES

- brush pens
- white card cut in a rectangle (6x8")
- a pencil, eraser, and ruler
- gel pens or felt pens

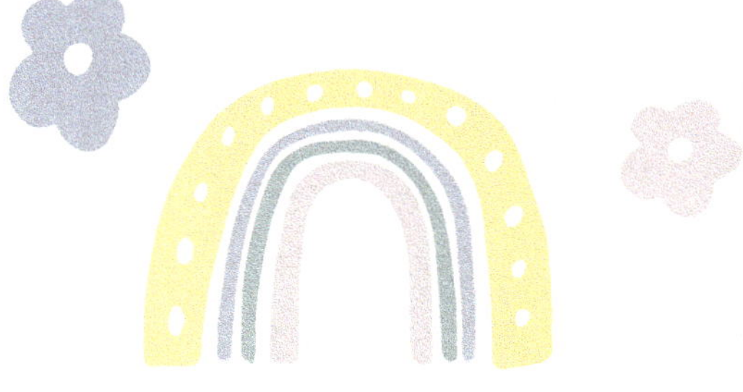

INSTRUCTIONS

1. Cut the cardboard into a rectangle. A 6x8" rectangle is a good size because then you can get a frame for it easily.

2. Choose the quote you would like to write. With the pencil and ruler, rule lines where the letters will go. With your pencil roughly write out the letters, making sure they are in the center of the page and nicely laid out. You can write some words in capital letters and some words in brush pen calligraphy.

You can also copy from the quotes on the next pages.

3. Use your brush pen to write the brush pen calligraphy words. Write the capitals in a gel pen or felt pen. You can choose some cheerful colours.

4. When you have finished the lettering, rub out the pencil lines.

5. Decorate your Wall Art with pictures or stickers, put it in a frame and enjoy!!!

Now move on to the next pages and practice some Wall Art.

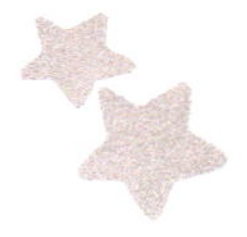

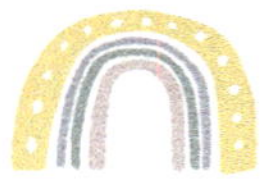

"BE SILLY, BE HUMBLE, BE KIND"

Practice the words below and then use the lay out of the quote on the next page to create your own Wall Art Poster. You can choose any colours you like and decorate it with your own pictures!

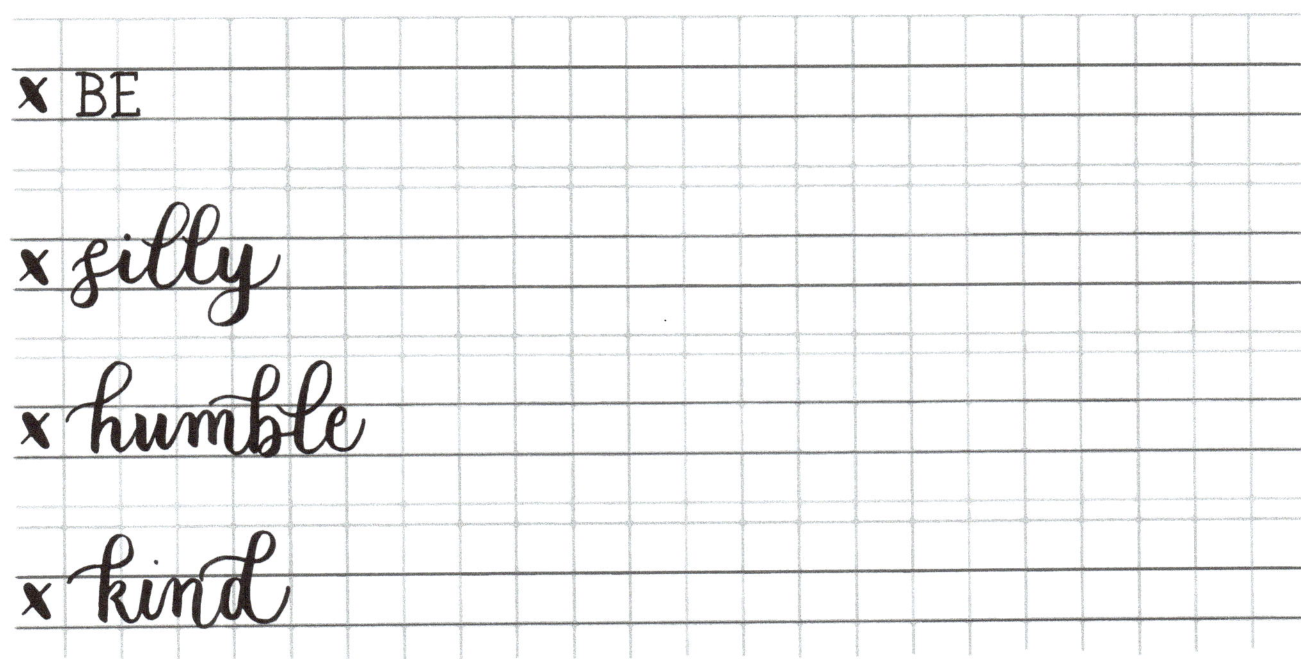

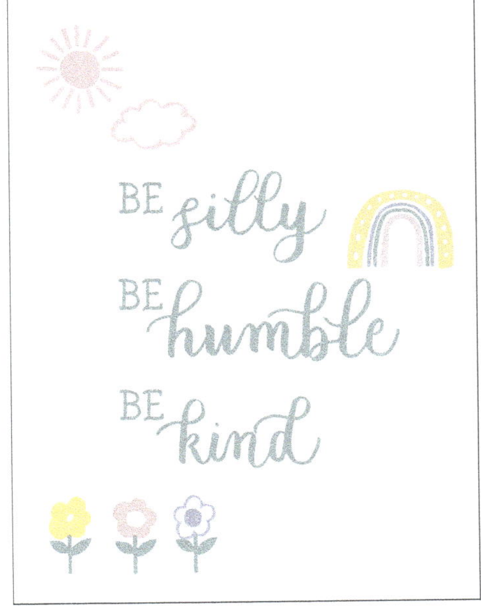

"BE SILLY, BE HUMBLE, BE KIND"

Use your brush pen calligraphy and felt pens to create this special wall art poster. What colour pens will you choose? You can decorate your wall art with lots of fun pictures too. Get creative and enjoy yourself!

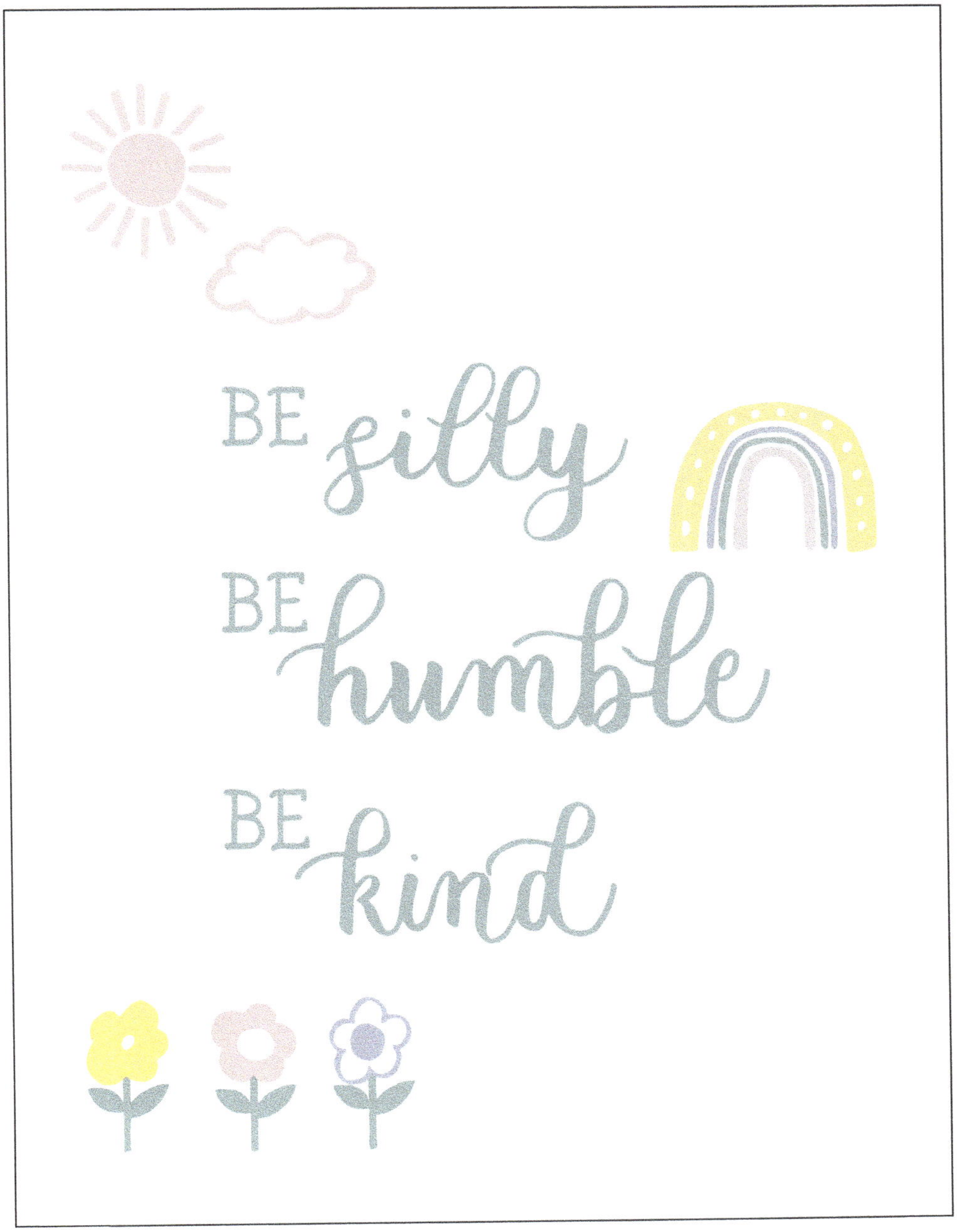

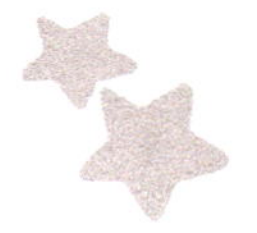

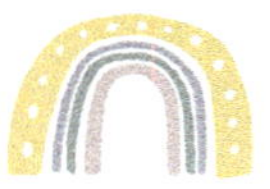

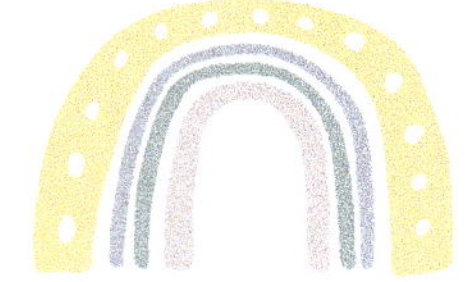

"EXPLORE, WONDER, CREATE"

Practice the words below and then use the lay out of the quote on the next page to create your own Wall Art Poster. You can choose any colours you like and decorate it with your own pictures!

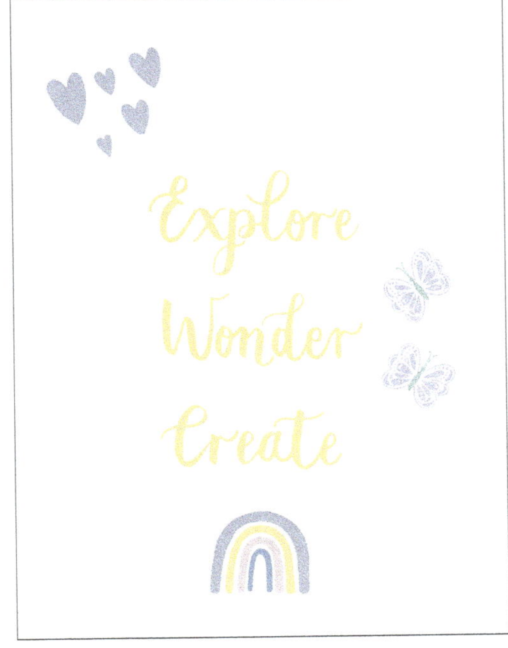

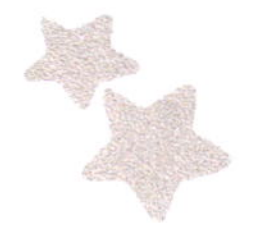

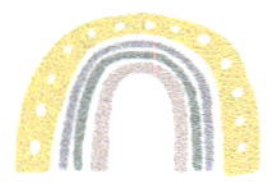

"EXPLORE, WONDER, CREATE"

Use your brush pen calligraphy and felt pens to create this special wall art poster. What colour pens will you choose? You can decorate your wall art with lots of fun pictures too. Get creative and enjoy yourself!

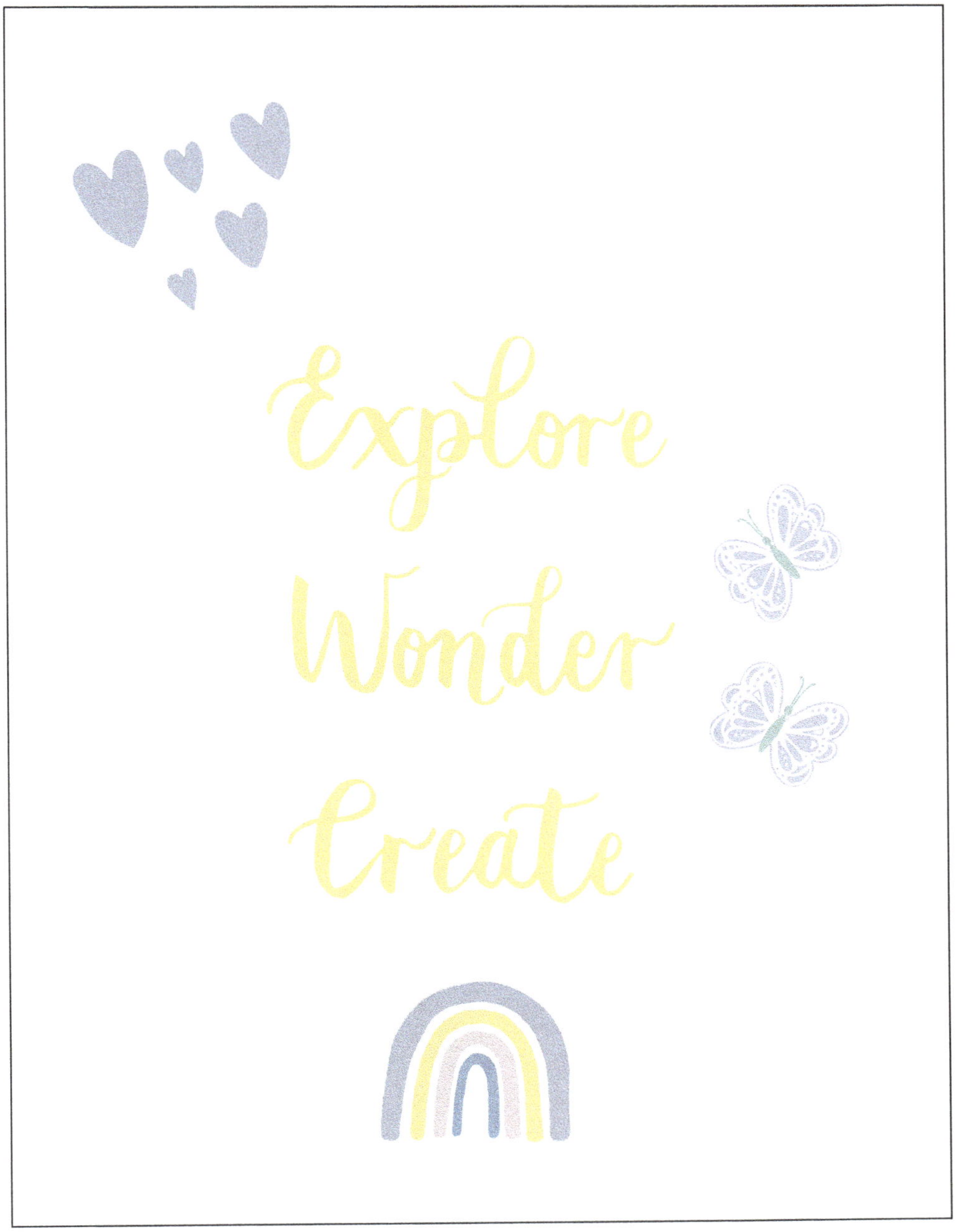

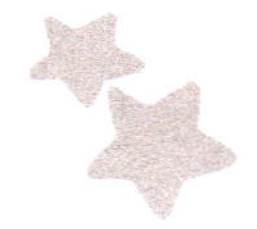
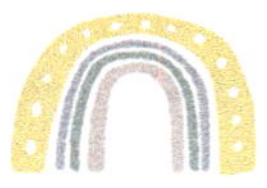

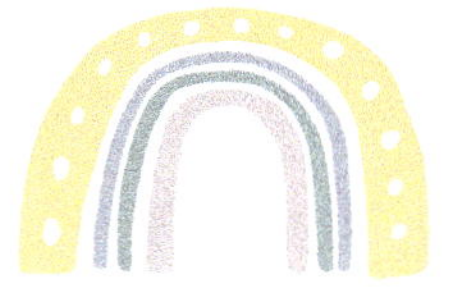

"YOU ARE AMAZING, YOU ARE BRAVE, YOU ARE STRONG"

Practice the words below and then use the lay out of the quote on the next page to create your own Wall Art Poster. You can choose any colours you like and decorate it with your own pictures!

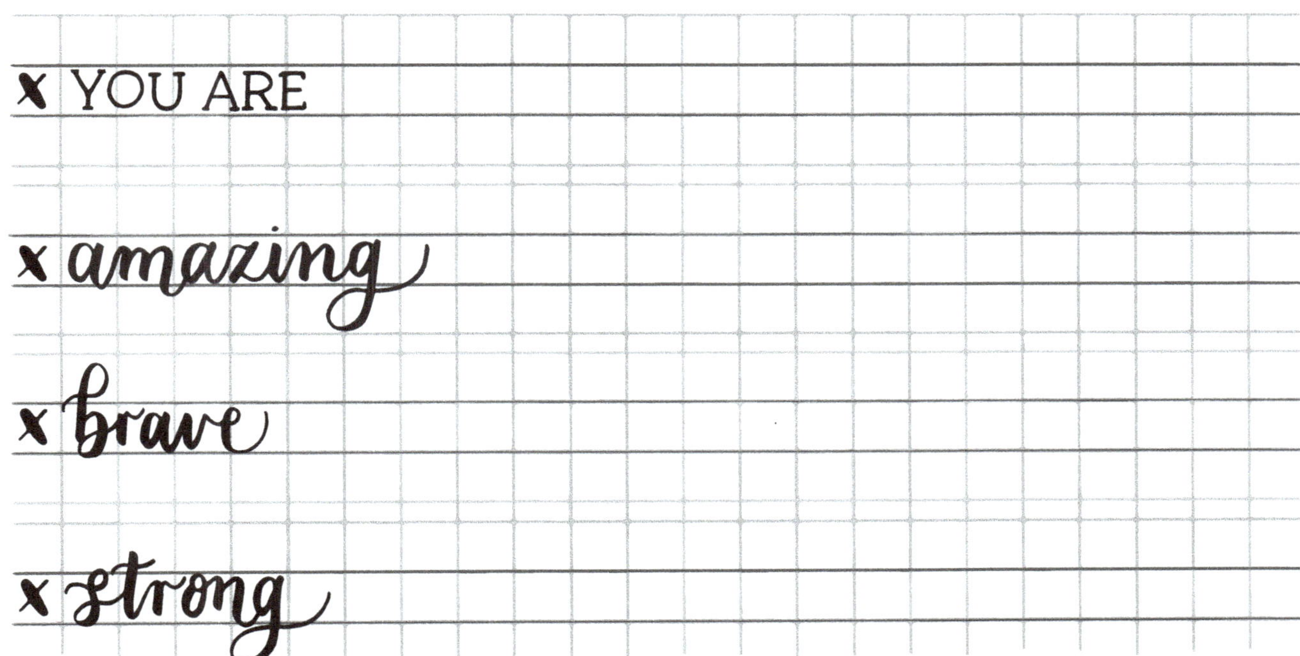

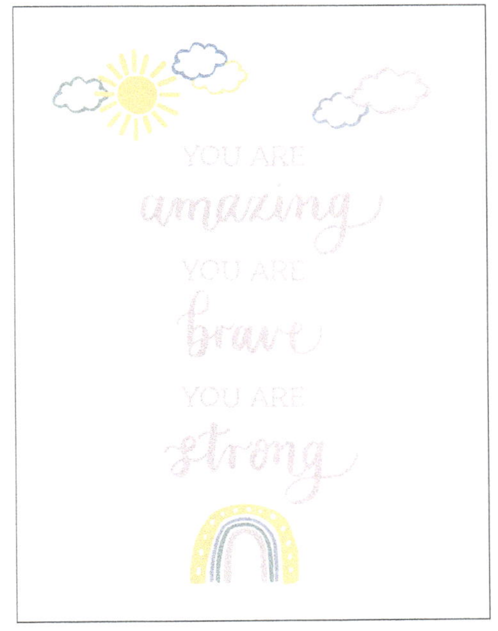

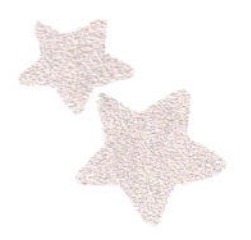 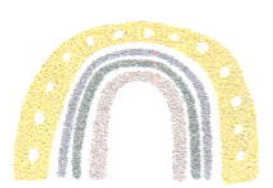

"YOU ARE AMAZING, YOU ARE BRAVE, YOU ARE STRONG"

Use your brush pen calligraphy and felt pens to create this special wall art poster. What colour pens will you choose? You can decorate your wall art with lots of fun pictures too. Get creative and enjoy yourself!

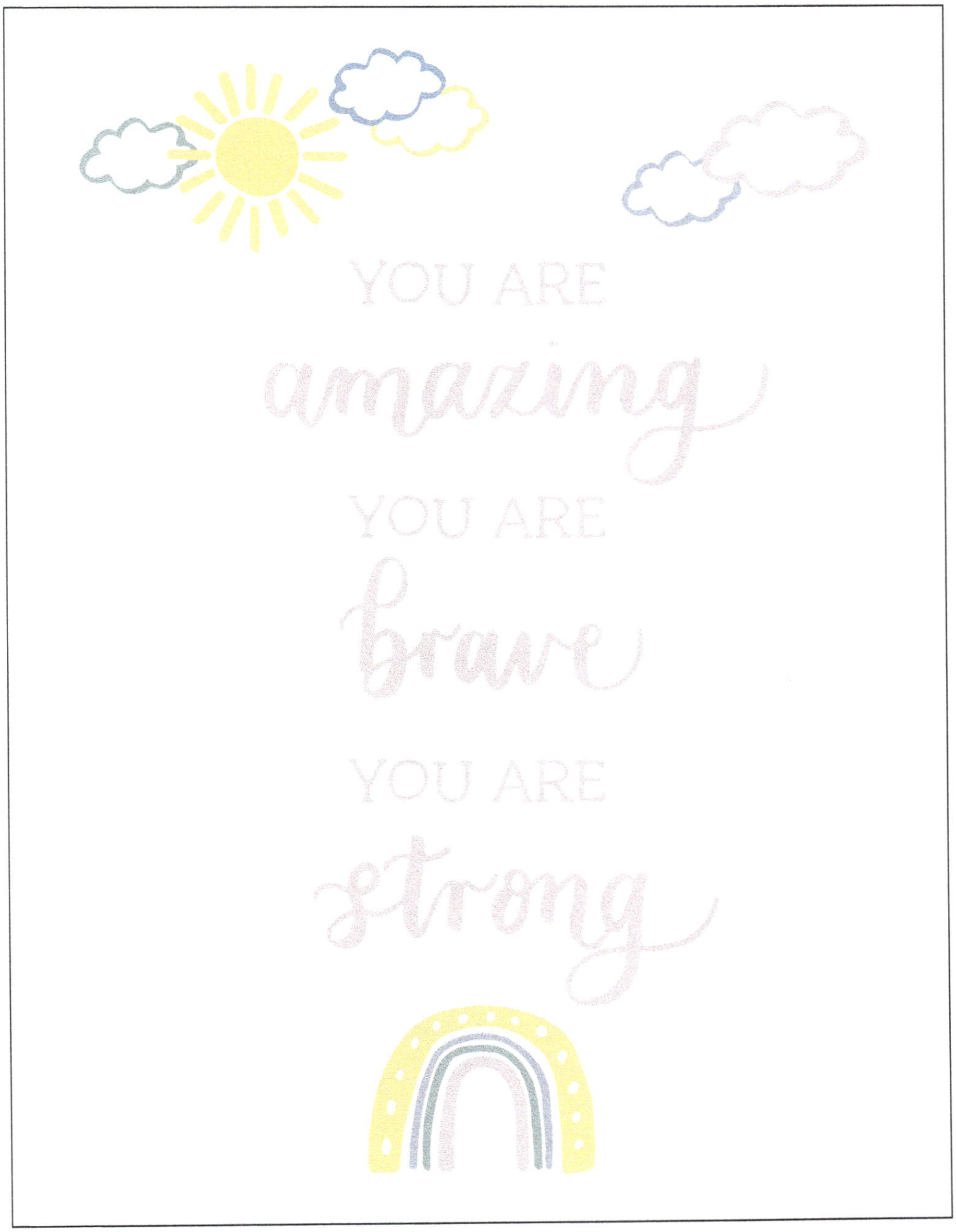

Practice the words below and then use the lay out of the quote on the next page to create your own Wall Art Poster. You can choose any colours you like and decorate it with your own pictures!

x WHEN IT

x rains

x LOOK FOR

x rainbows

x WHEN IT'S

x dark

x LOOK FOR

x stars

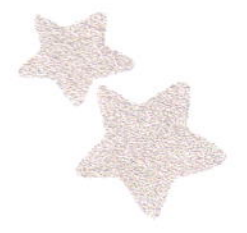

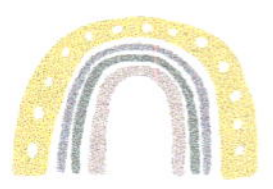

Use your brush pen calligraphy and felt pens to create this special wall art poster. What colour pens will you choose? You can decorate your wall art with lots of fun pictures too. Get creative and enjoy yourself!

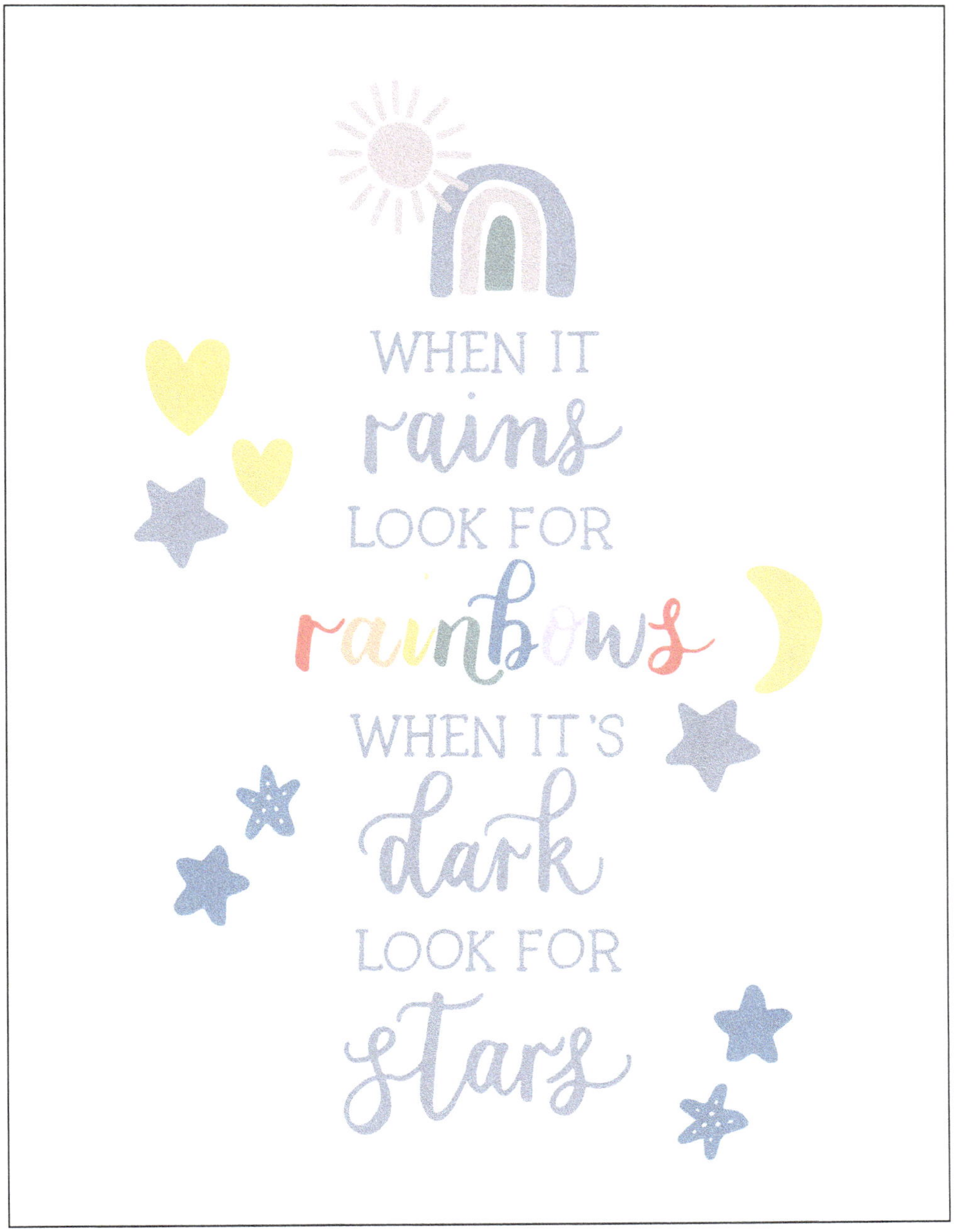

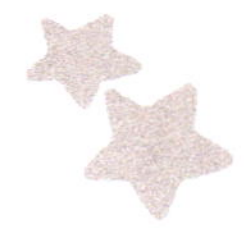

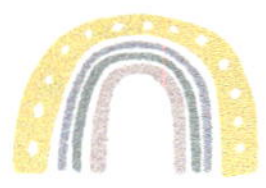

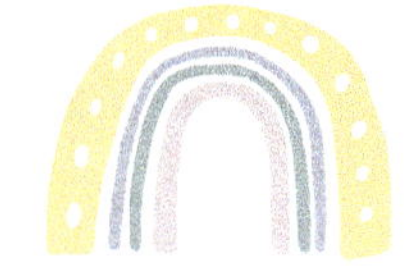

"BE A UNICORN IN A FIELD OF HORSES"

Practice the words below and then use the lay out of the quote on the next page to create your own Wall Art Poster. You can choose any colours you like and decorate it with your own pictures!

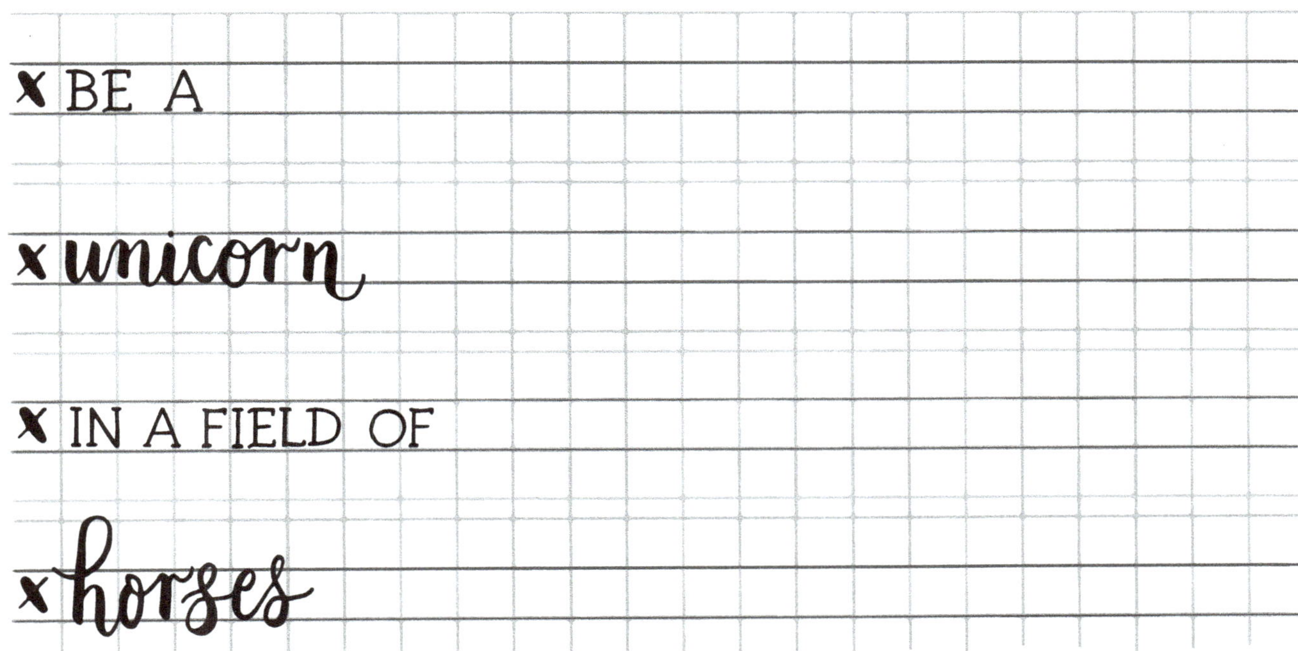

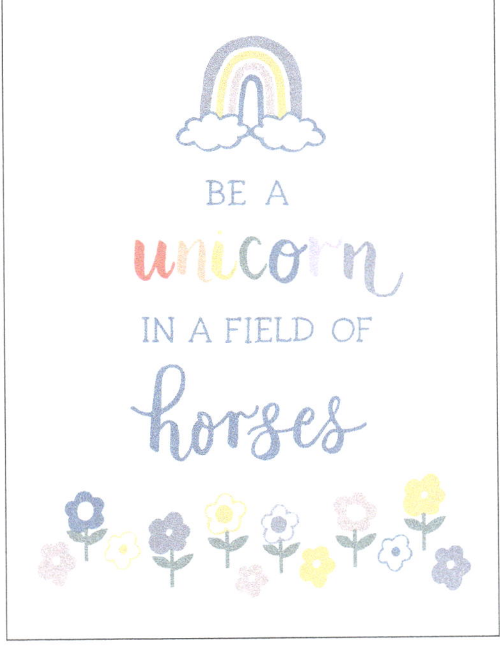

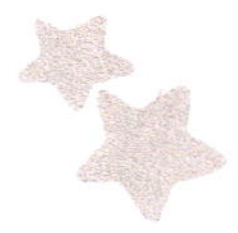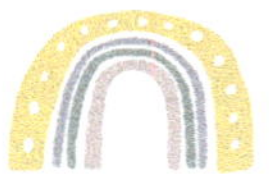

WALL ART EXAMPLE

"BE A UNICORN IN A FIELD OF HORSES"

Use your brush pen calligraphy and felt pens to create this special wall art poster. What colour pens will you choose? You can decorate your wall art with lots of fun pictures too. Get creative and enjoy yourself!

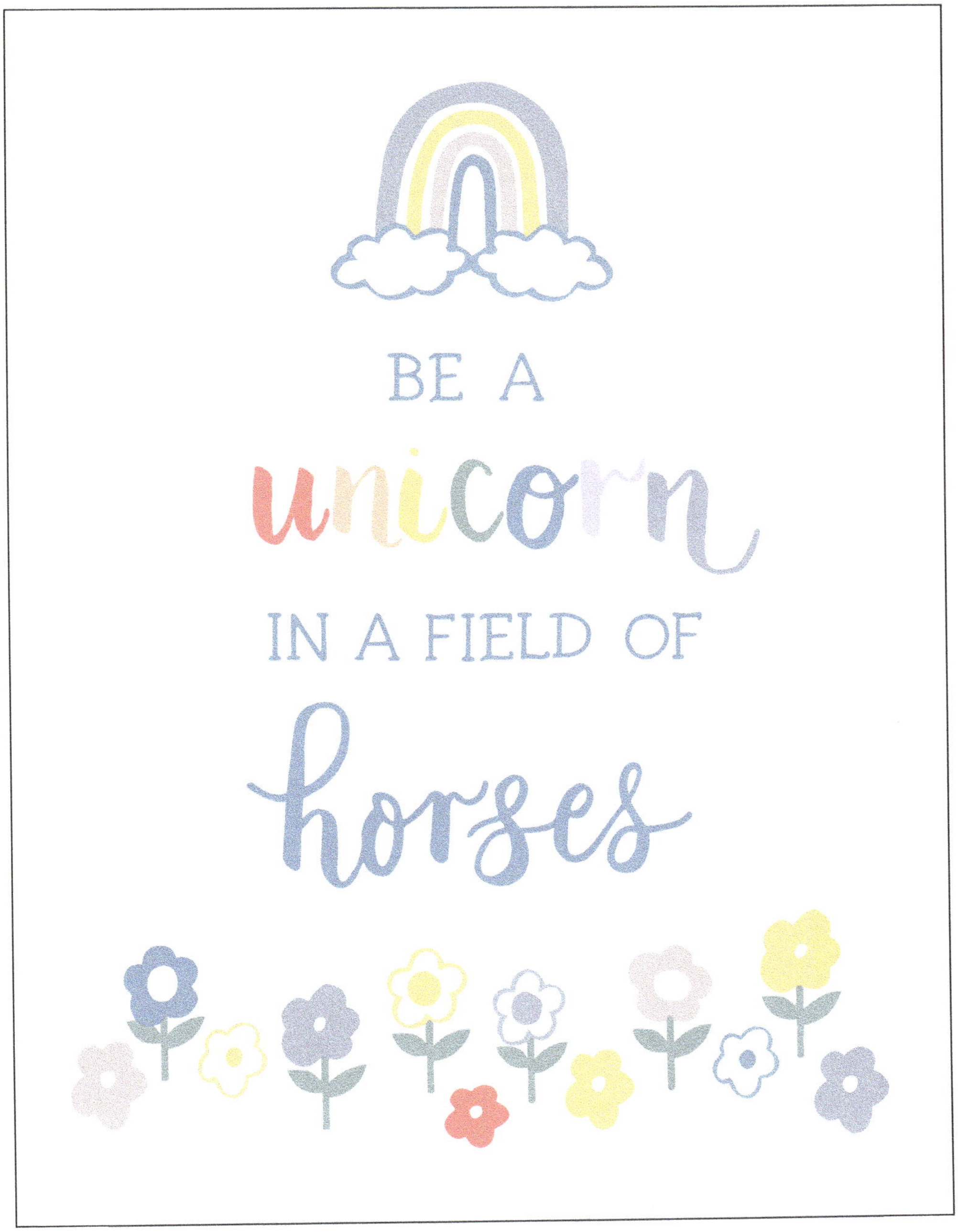

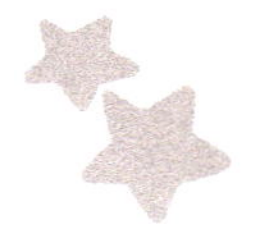
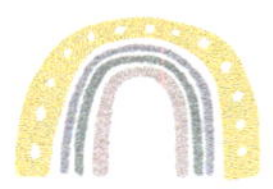

Kids Calligraphy

MAKING A WALL ART QUOTE

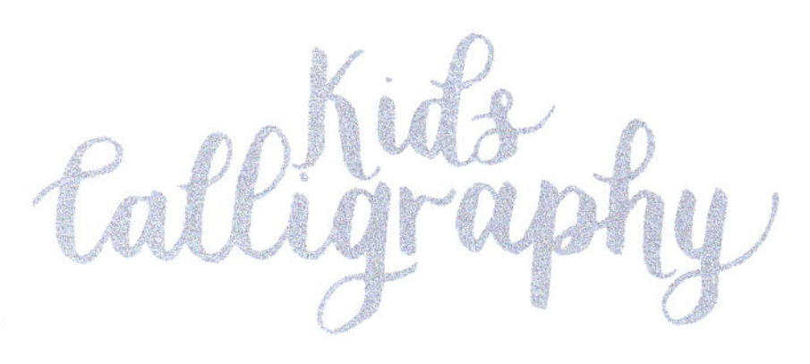

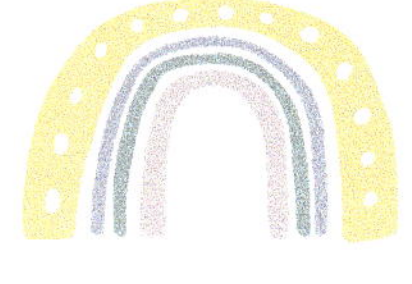

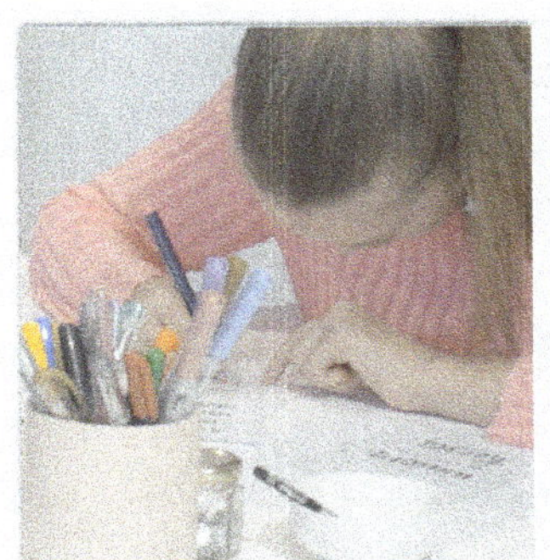

Practicing the brush pen calligraphy lettering for the quote.

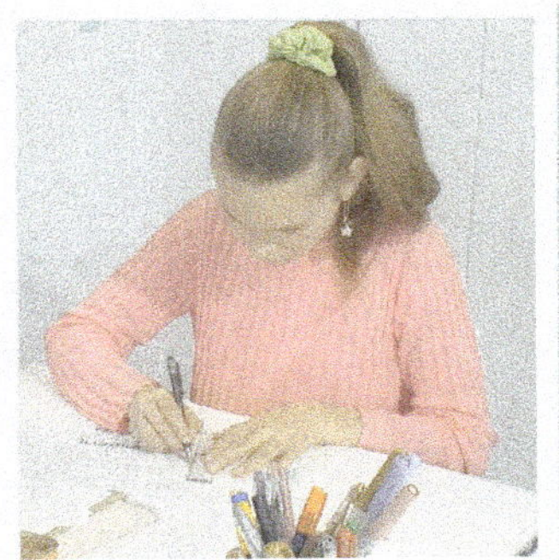

Ruling lines and writing the letters in pencil.

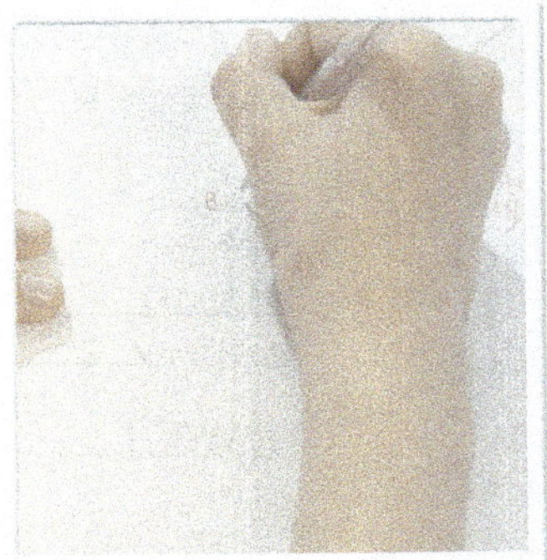

Writing the capital letters using a gel pen.

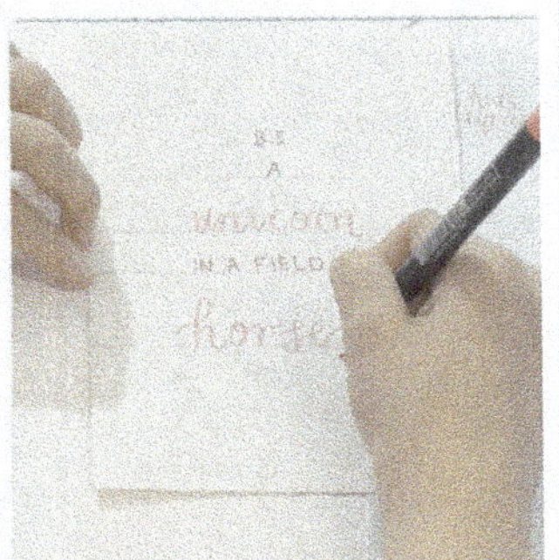

Writing the brush pen calligraphy

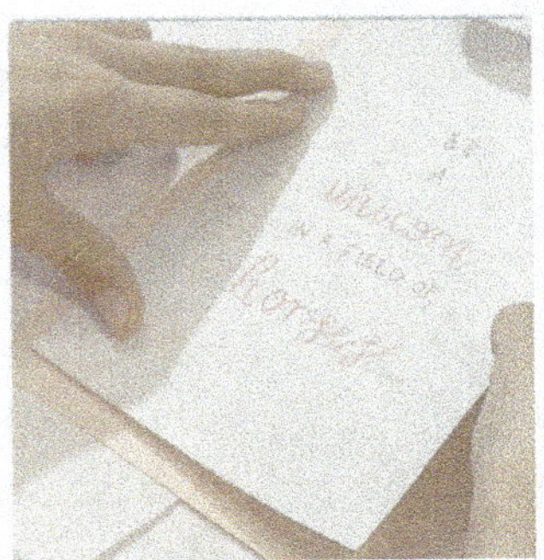

Gluing the Wall Art quote onto a card background.

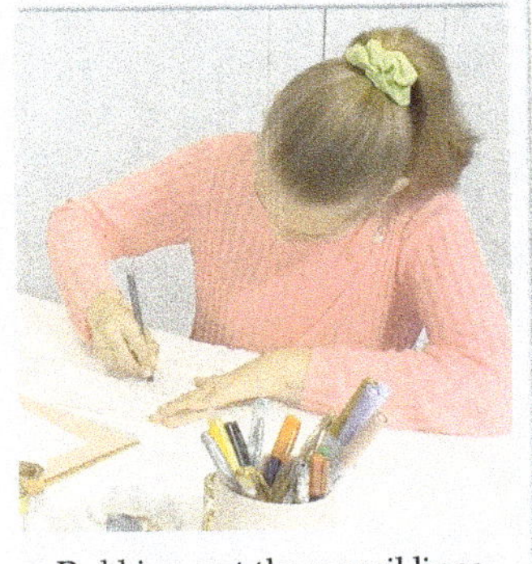

Rubbing out the pencil lines.

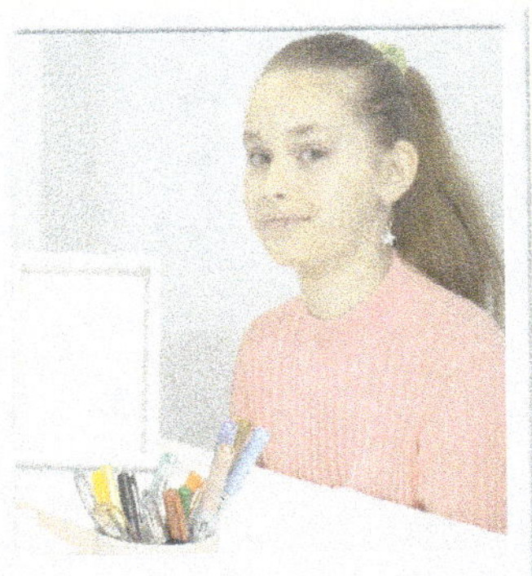

Putting the Wall Art in a frame and voila! It's finished.

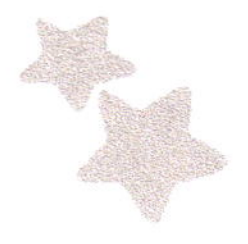

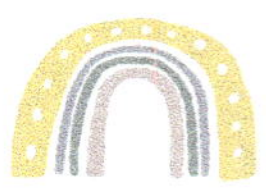

Create your very own greeting cards to give to family or friends on special occasions.
Use your Brush Pen Calligraphy to make a card and also write the person's name on the
envelope! You can choose your own special greeting to letter and decorate. Or you can use
the greeting card templates on the next few pages.

SUPPLIES

- brush pens
- white card cut and folded to fit an envelope
- a pencil and ruler
- an envelope
- optional decorations: wax seal, gold flakes/glitter,
   or stickers

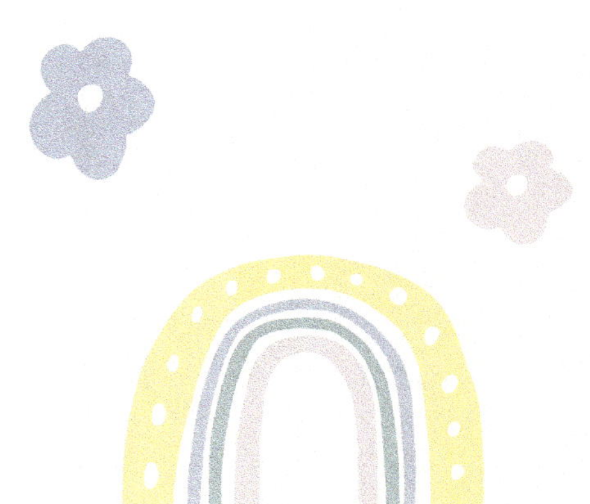

INSTRUCTIONS

1. Cut the cardboard into double the envelope size and fold the card in half. For example,
for a card to fit a 5x7" envelope cut the card to 10"x 7" and fold in half.

2. Choose the greeting that you would like to write. With the pencil and ruler, rule lines
where the letters will go. With your pencil roughly write the letters, making sure they
are in the center of the card and nicely laid out. You can practice the greeting words
from the greeting cards practice sheet and the layouts on the next pages.

3. Use your brush pen to write the brush pen calligraphy words. You can choose some
cheerful colours.

4. When you have finished the lettering, rub out the pencil lines.

5. You can decorate the card with pictures, or stickers. Or you can put a little bit of glue
on the card and add glitter or gold flakes.

6. Write the name of the person you are giving the card to on the front of the
envelope. Place the card inside. You can add a wax seal to the envelope for an extra
special decoration.

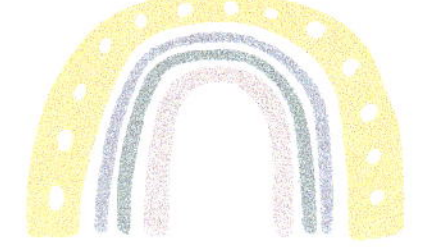

Practice the words below. There is some extra space on the next page to practice too. Then you can use the lay out of the greeting cards on the pages after that to create your own greeting cards. You can choose any colours you like and decorate it with your own pictures!

x Happy Birthday

x Happy Mother's Day

x Happy Father's Day

x Happy New Year

x Merry Christmas

x Thank you

x I love you

Use the extra space below to practice the greeting card words. Then you can start to make your own greeting cards. Use the next few pages as inspiration!

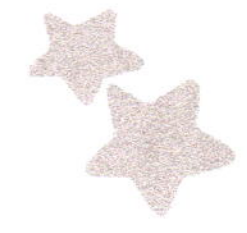

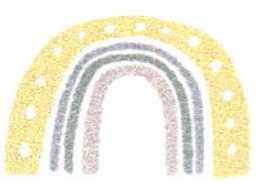

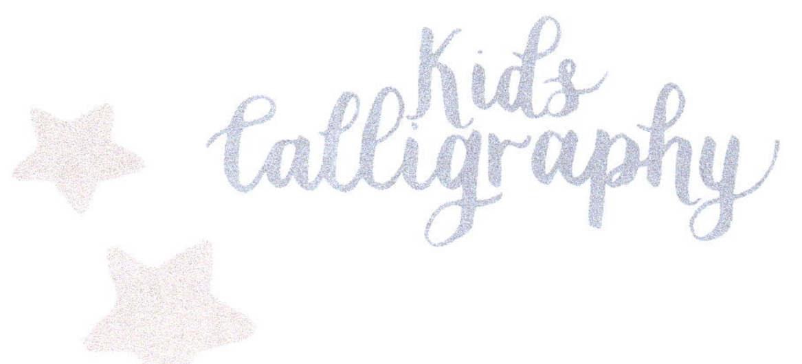

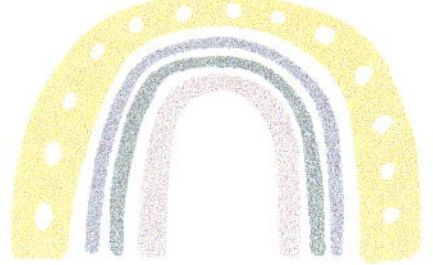

Use your brush pen calligraphy to create this special greeting card. What colour pens will you choose? You can decorate your greeting card with lots of fun pictures too. Or you can add glitter and stickers. Get creative and enjoy yourself!

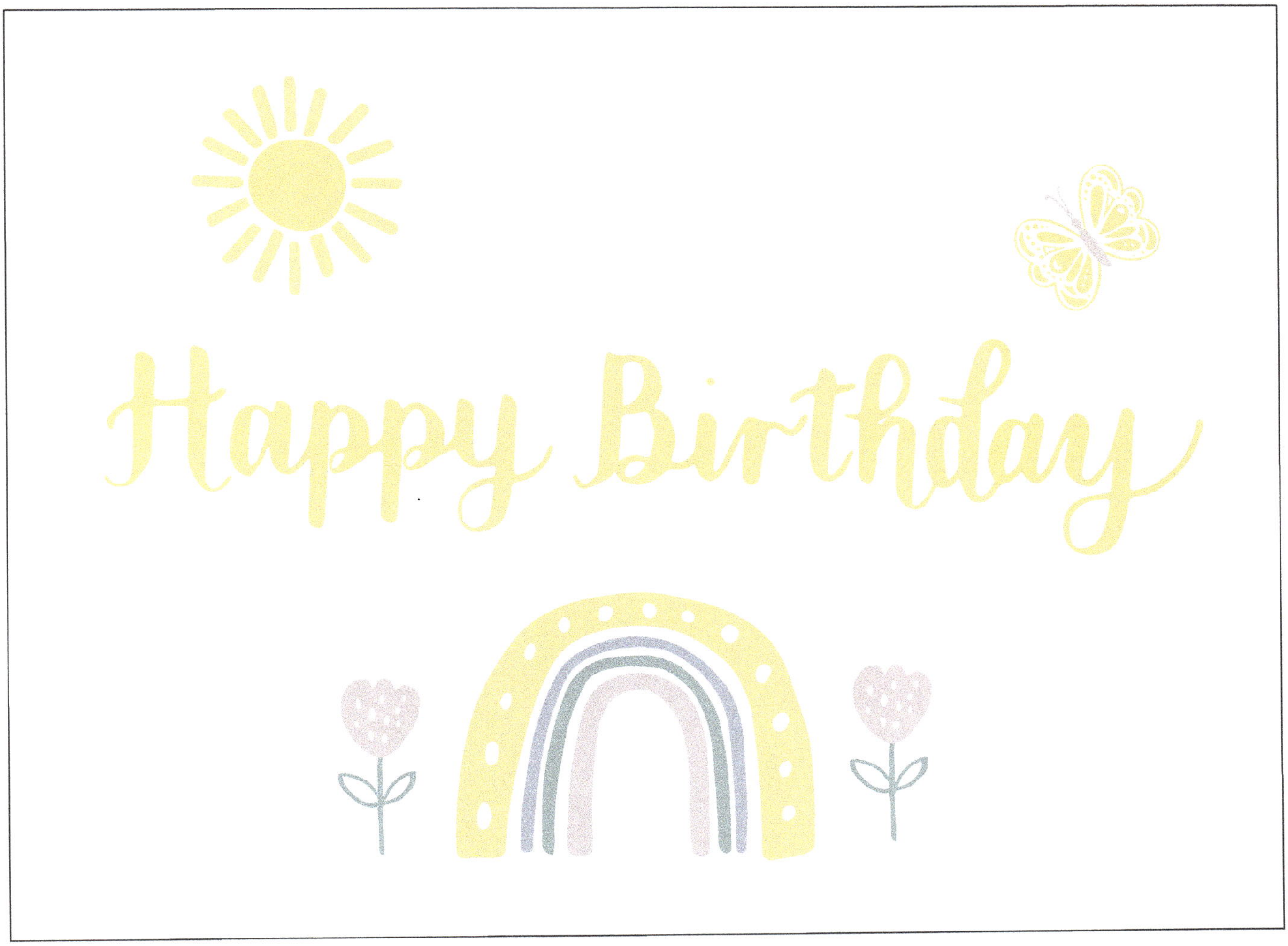

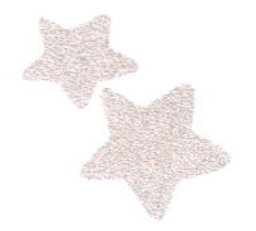

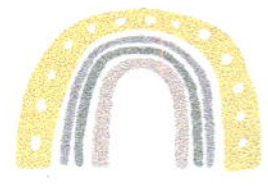

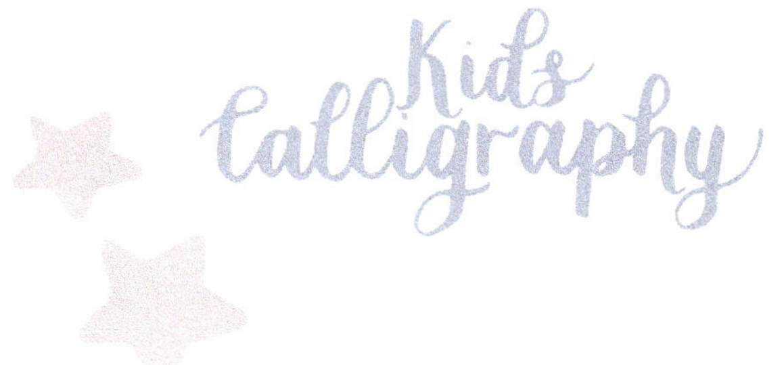 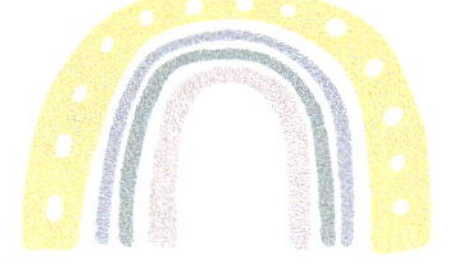

Use your brush pen calligraphy to create this special greeting card. What colour pens will you choose? You can decorate your greeting card with lots of fun pictures too. Or you can add glitter and stickers. Get creative and enjoy yourself!

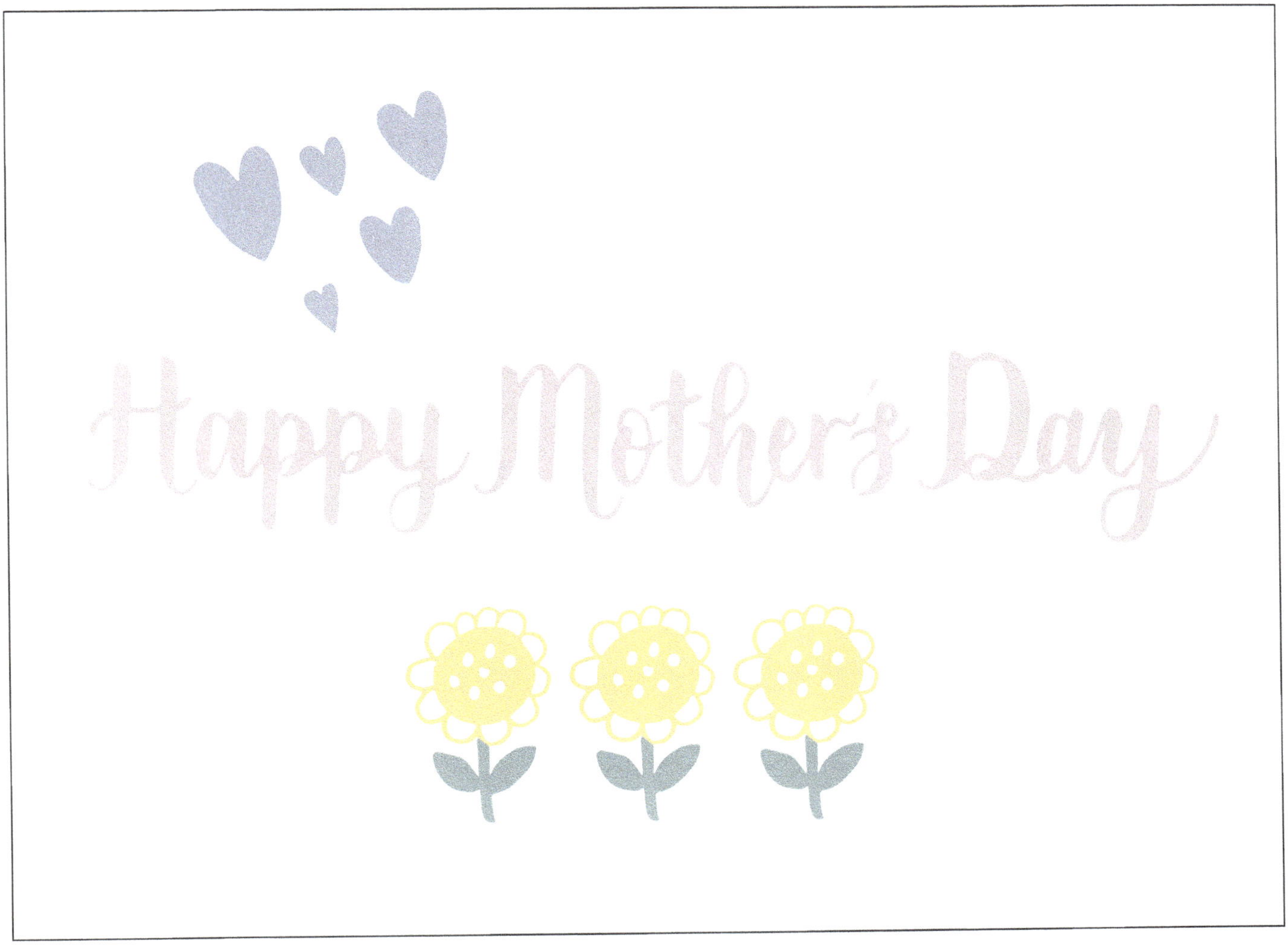

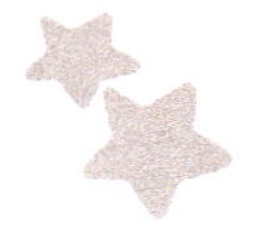
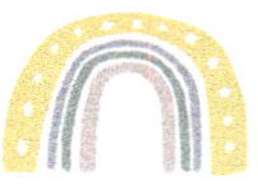

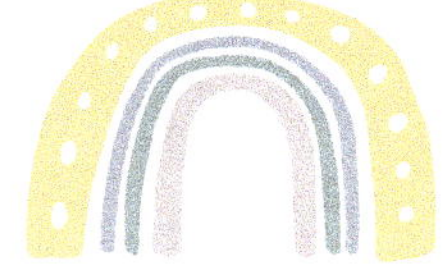

Use your brush pen calligraphy to create this special greeting card. What colour pens
will you choose? You can decorate your greeting card with lots of fun pictures too.
Or you can add glitter and stickers. Get creative and enjoy yourself!

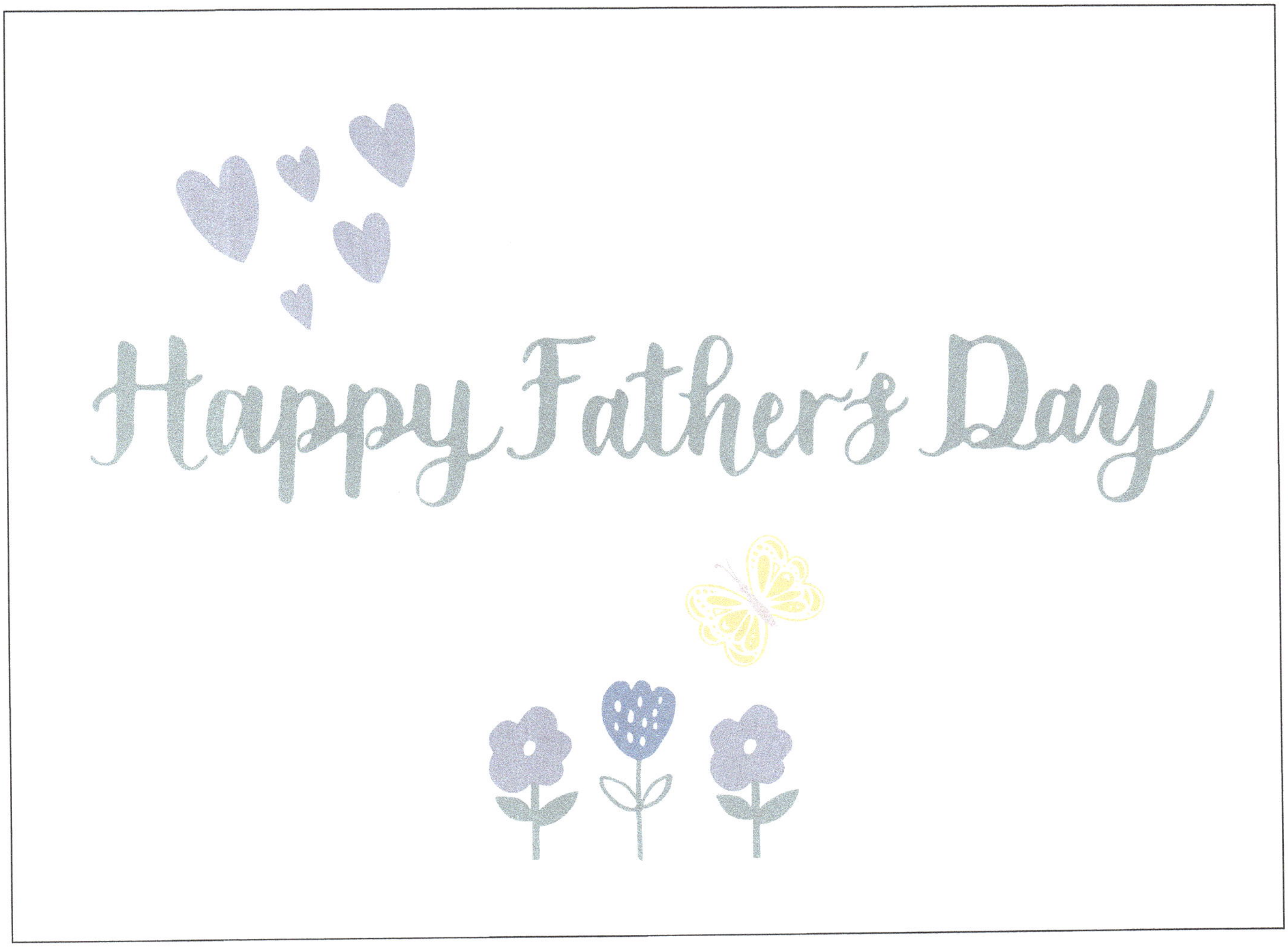

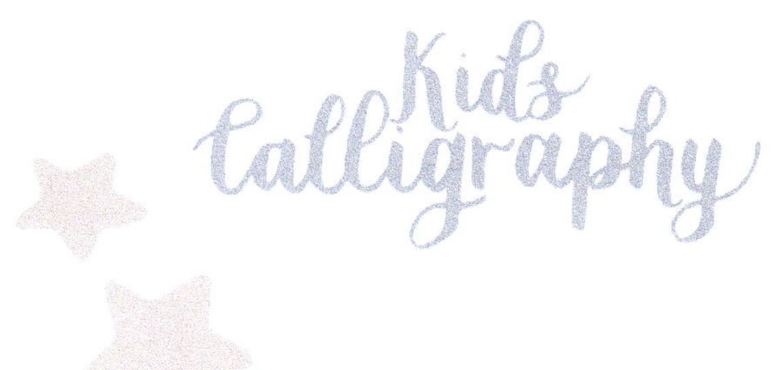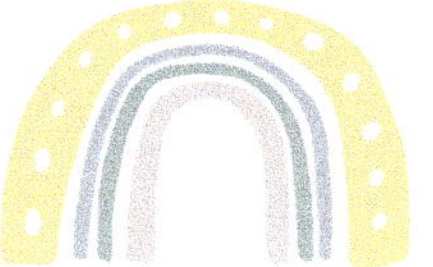

GREETING CARD EXAMPLE

Use your brush pen calligraphy to create this special greeting card. What colour pens will you choose? You can decorate your greeting card with lots of fun pictures too. Or you can add glitter and stickers. Get creative and enjoy yourself!

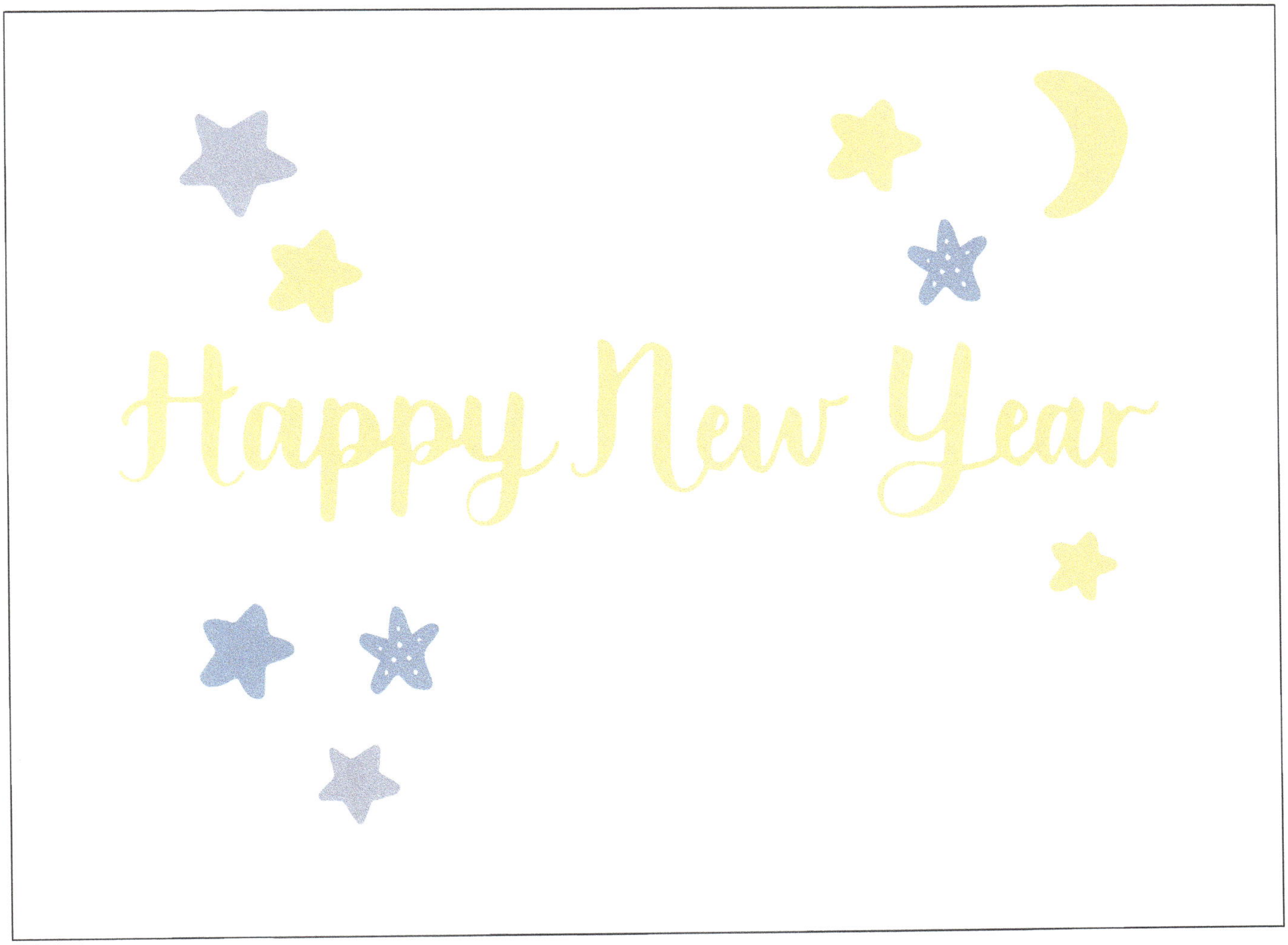

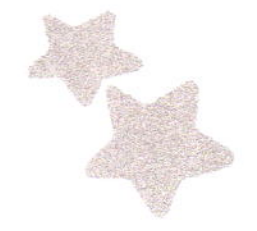
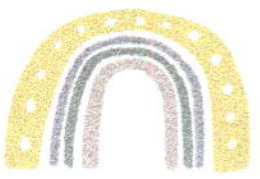

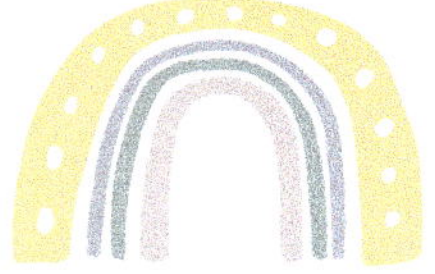

Use your brush pen calligraphy to create this special greeting card. What colour pens will you choose? You can decorate your greeting card with lots of fun pictures too. Or you can add glitter and stickers. Get creative and enjoy yourself!

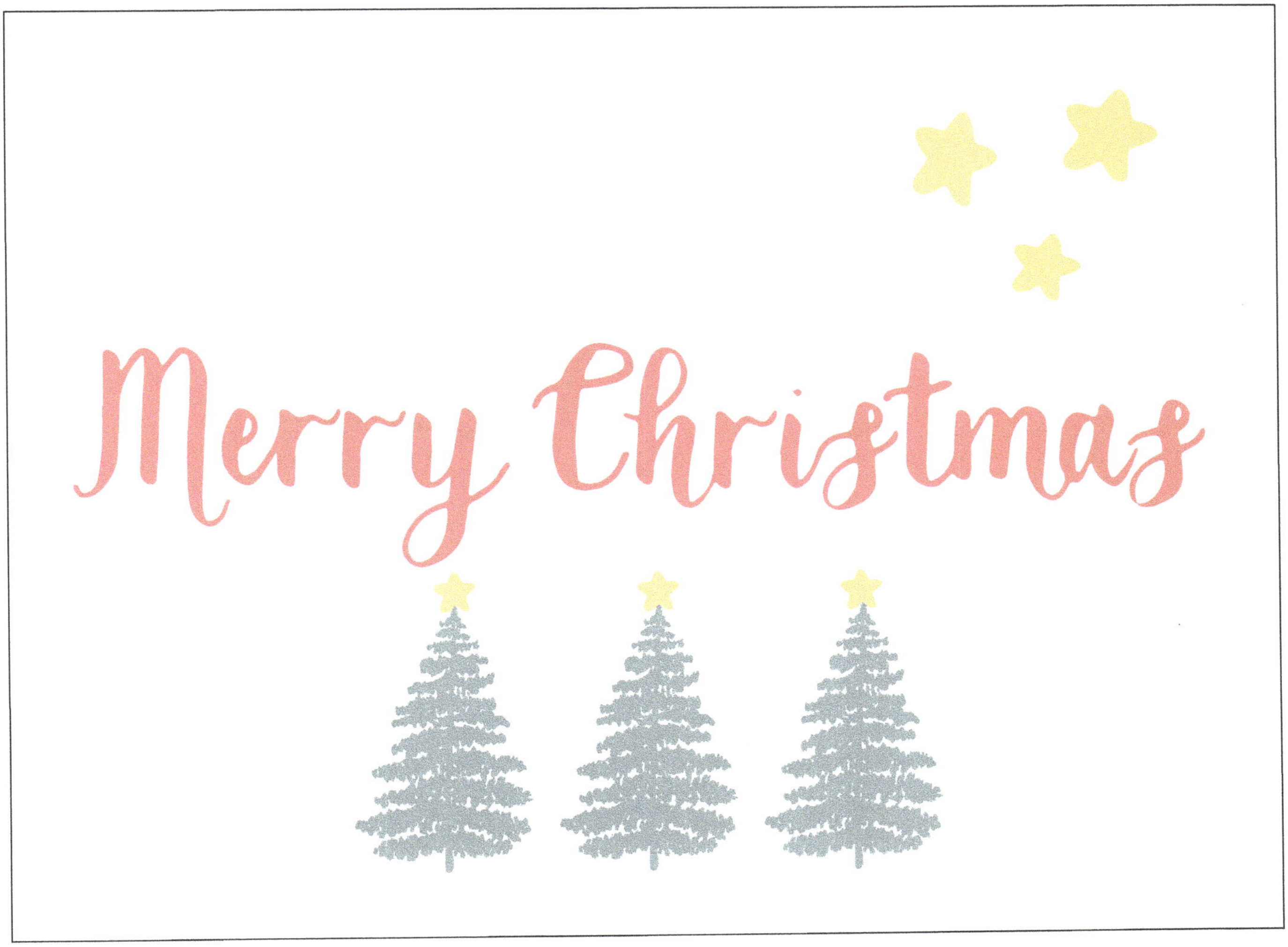

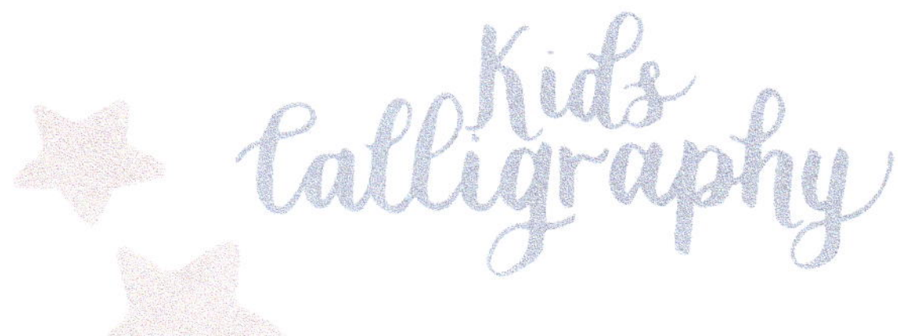

GREETING CARD EXAMPLE

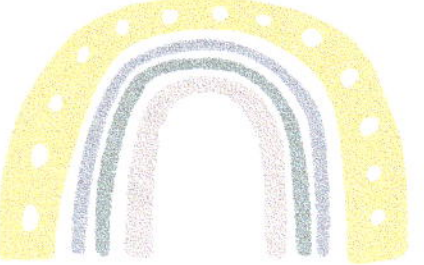

Use your brush pen calligraphy to create this special greeting card. What colour pens will you choose? You can decorate your greeting card with lots of fun pictures too. Or you can add glitter and stickers. Get creative and enjoy yourself!

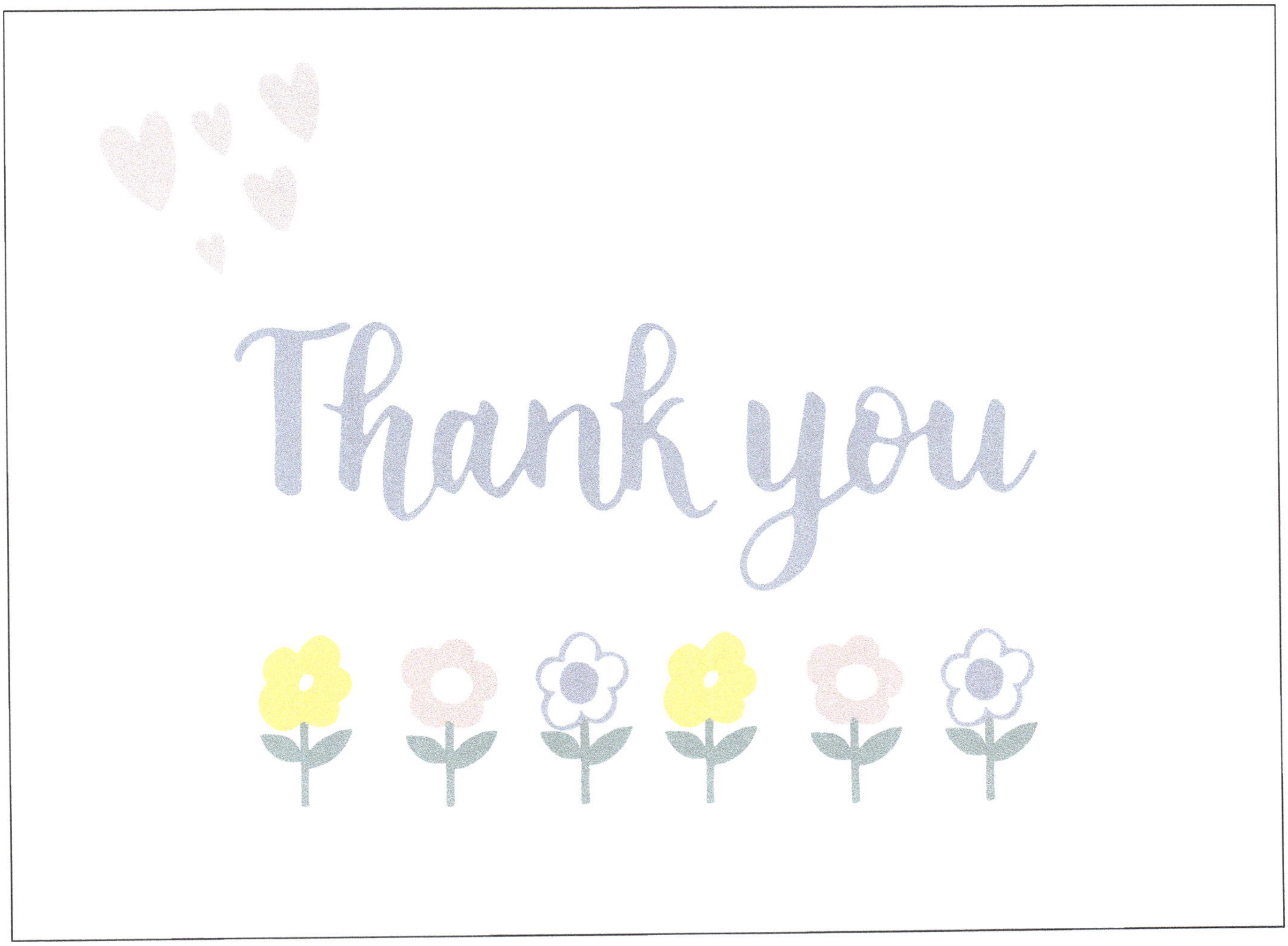

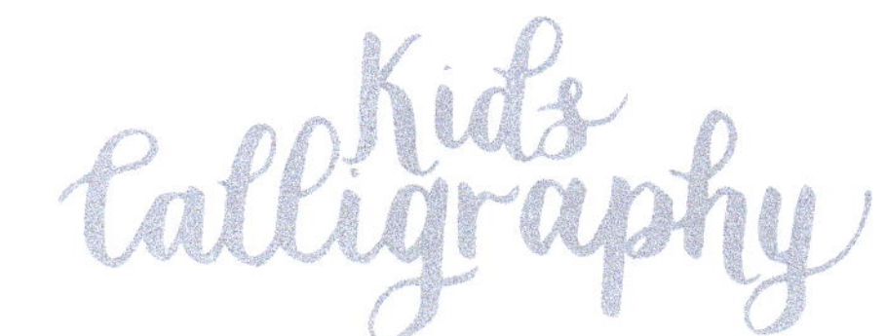 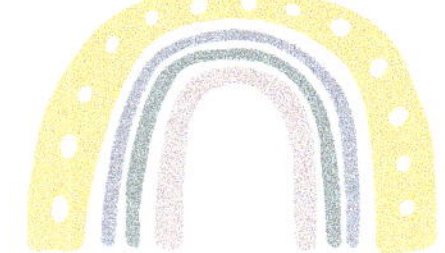

GREETING CARD EXAMPLE

Use your brush pen calligraphy to create this special greeting card. What colour pens will you choose? You can decorate your greeting card with lots of fun pictures too. Or you can add glitter and stickers. Get creative and enjoy yourself!

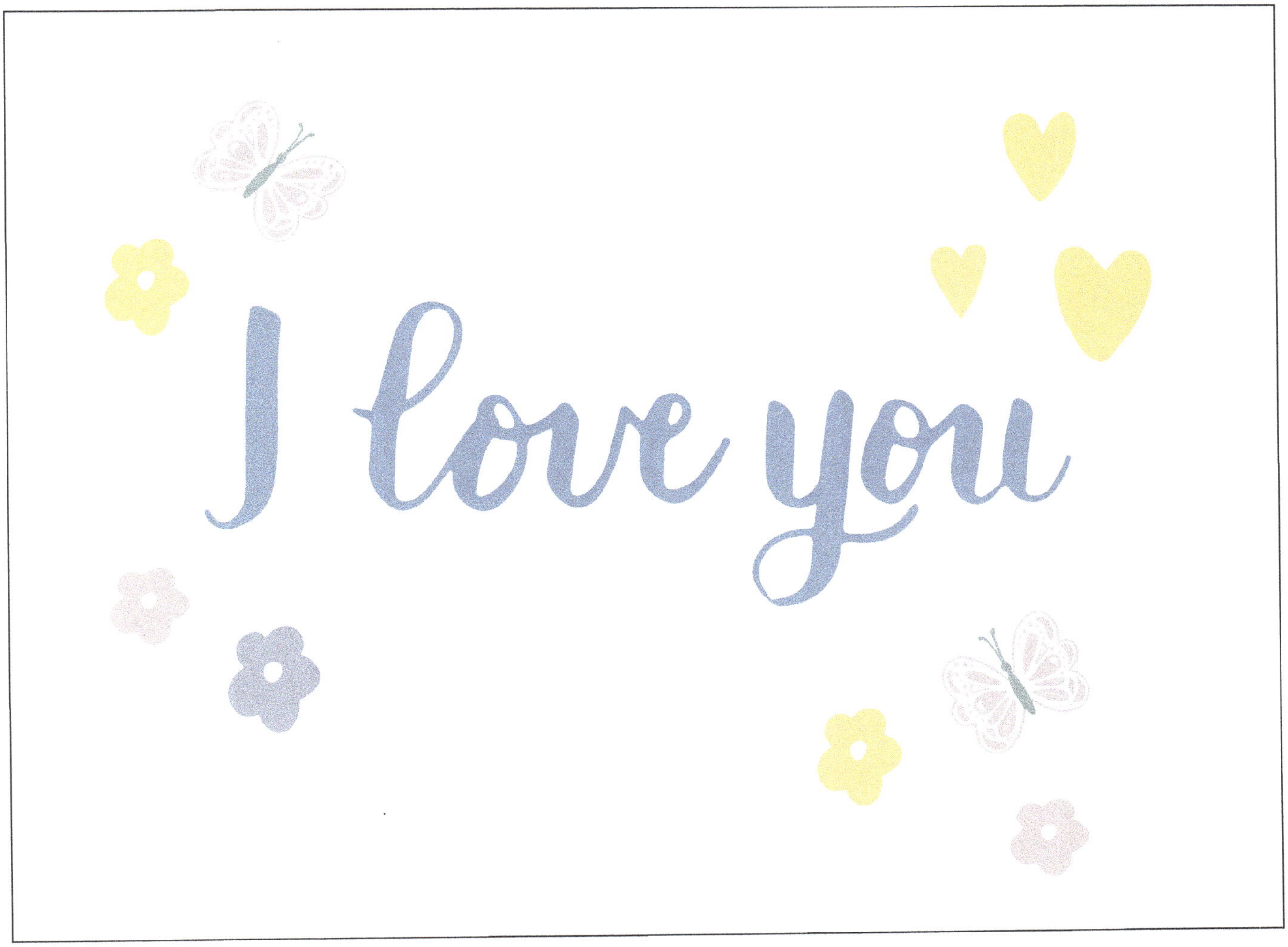

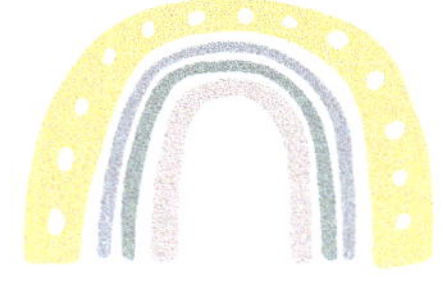

MAKING A GREETING CARD

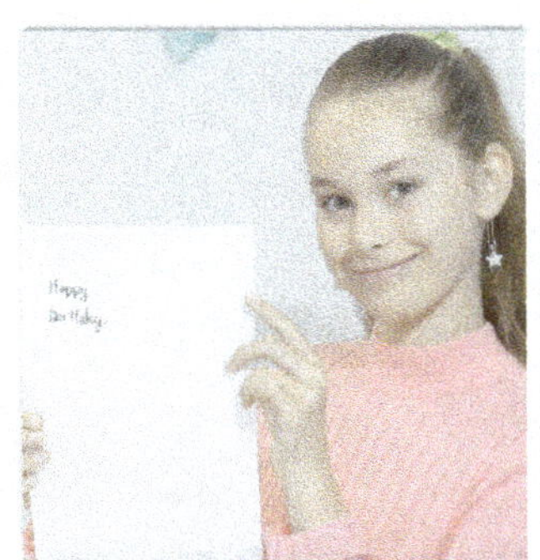

Practicing the brush pen calligraphy for the greeting card.

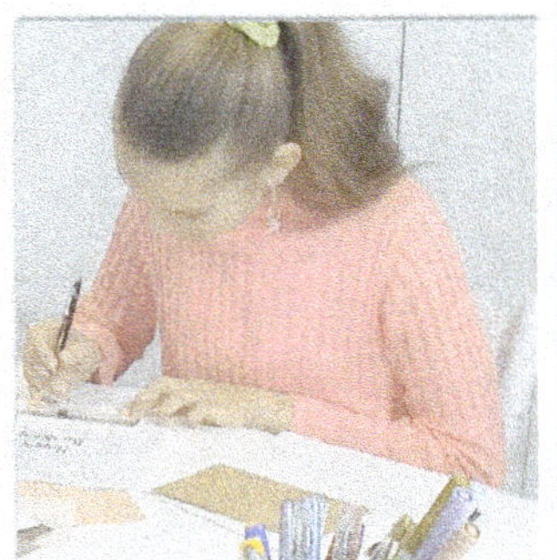

Ruling lines and writing the letters in pencil.

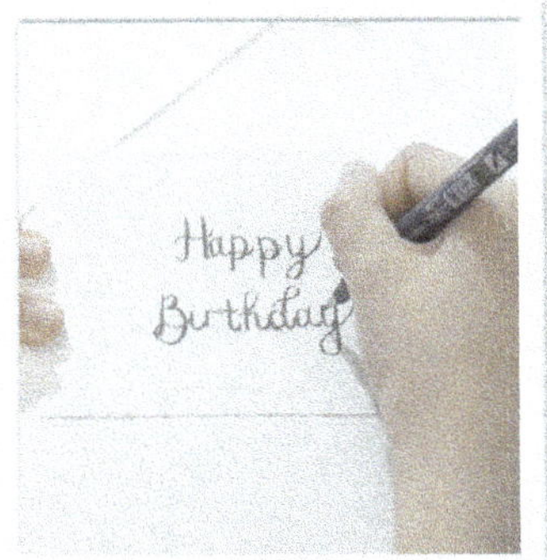

Writing the brush pen calligraphy words on the card.

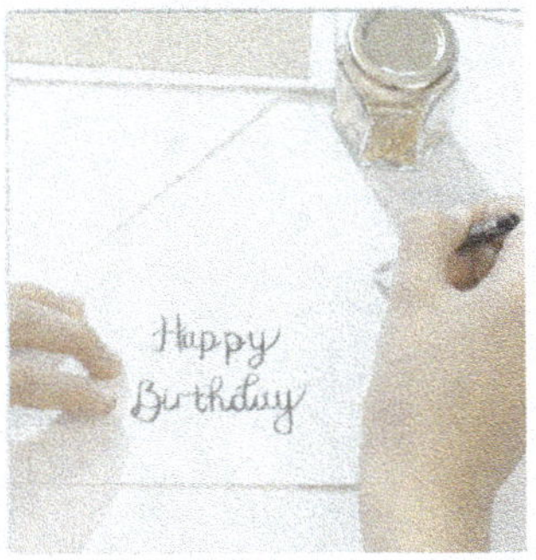

Putting glue on the corners of the card.

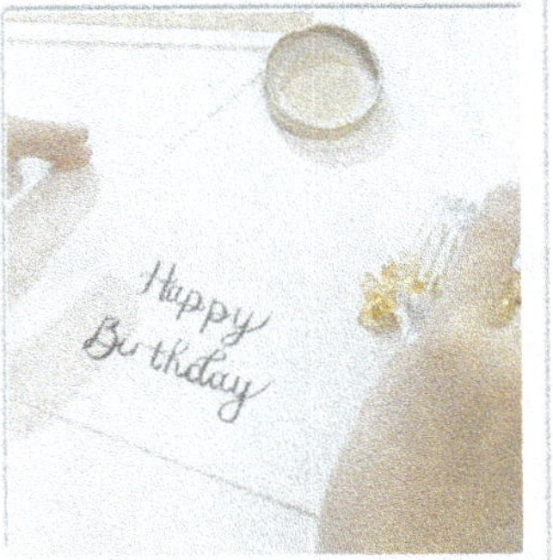

Putting some gold leaf on the glue to decorate the card.

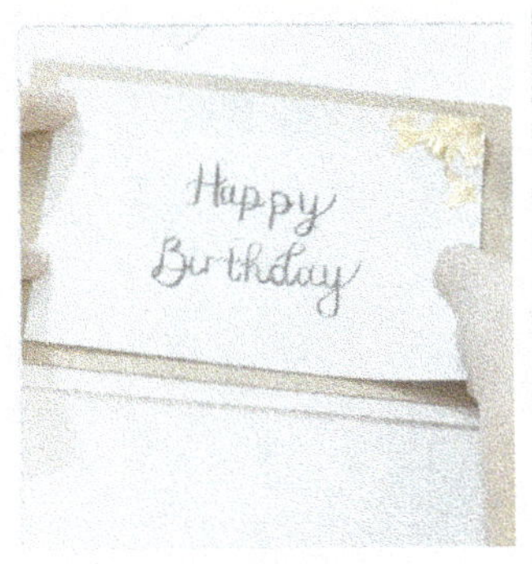

Putting the card onto a coloured background.

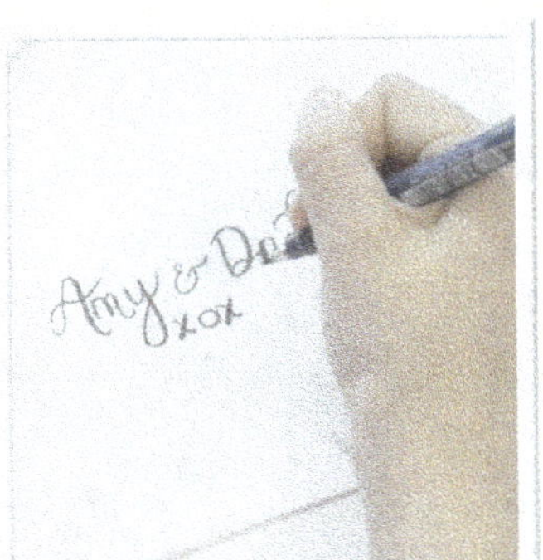

Writing the names on the front of the envelope.

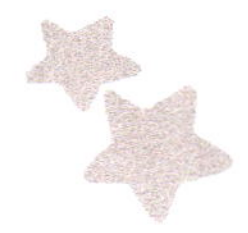

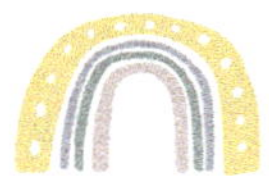

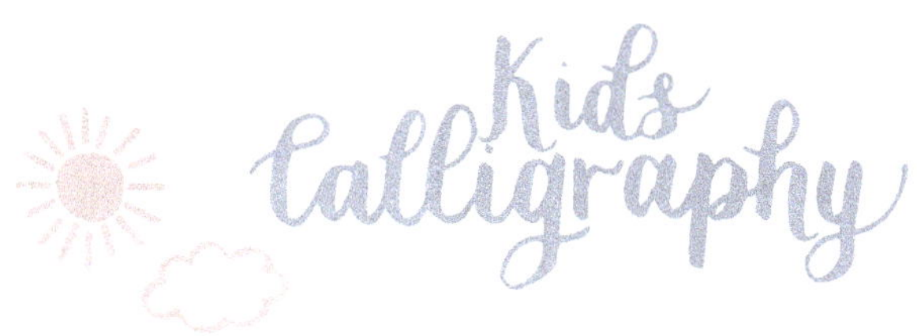

Create your very own piece of art you can use while reading. Use your Brush Pen Calligraphy to make a bookmark! Choose your own special book quotes to letter and decorate. You can use your bookmark in your own books or make a lovely bookmark as a gift for a friend.

To practice your lettering, you can copy the special bookmark quotes on the next few pages.

SUPPLIES

- brush pens
- white card cut into a bookmark size (2″ x 8″)
- a pencil, an eraser, and ruler
- gel pens or felt pens
- a hole punch
- ribbon or a tassle

INSTRUCTIONS

1. Cut the cardboard into a bookmark size. A 2″x 8″ rectangle is a good size because it will fit into your book easily.

2. Choose the book quote you would like to write. With the pencil and ruler, rule lines where the letters will go. With your pencil roughly write out the letters, making sure they are in the center of the bookmark and nicely laid out. You can write some words in capital letters and some words in brush pen calligraphy. You can also copy from the quotes about books on the next pages.

3. Use your brush pen to write the brush pen calligraphy words. Write the capitals in a gel pen or felt pen. You can choose some cheerful colours.

4. When you have finished the lettering, rub out the pencil lines.

5. Punch a hole in the top of the bookmarkand tie a ribbon or tassle through the hole. Enjoy reading your book!

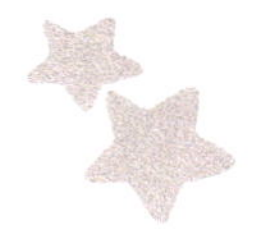

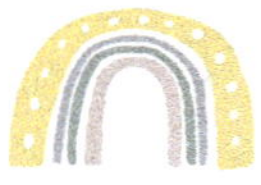

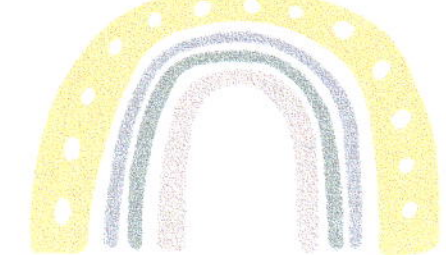

"BOOKS ARE PORTABLE MAGIC"

Practice the words below and then use the lay out of the book quotes on the next pages to create your own bookmark. You can choose any colours you like and decorate it with your own pictures! Remember to add a ribbon or tassle to your bookmark.

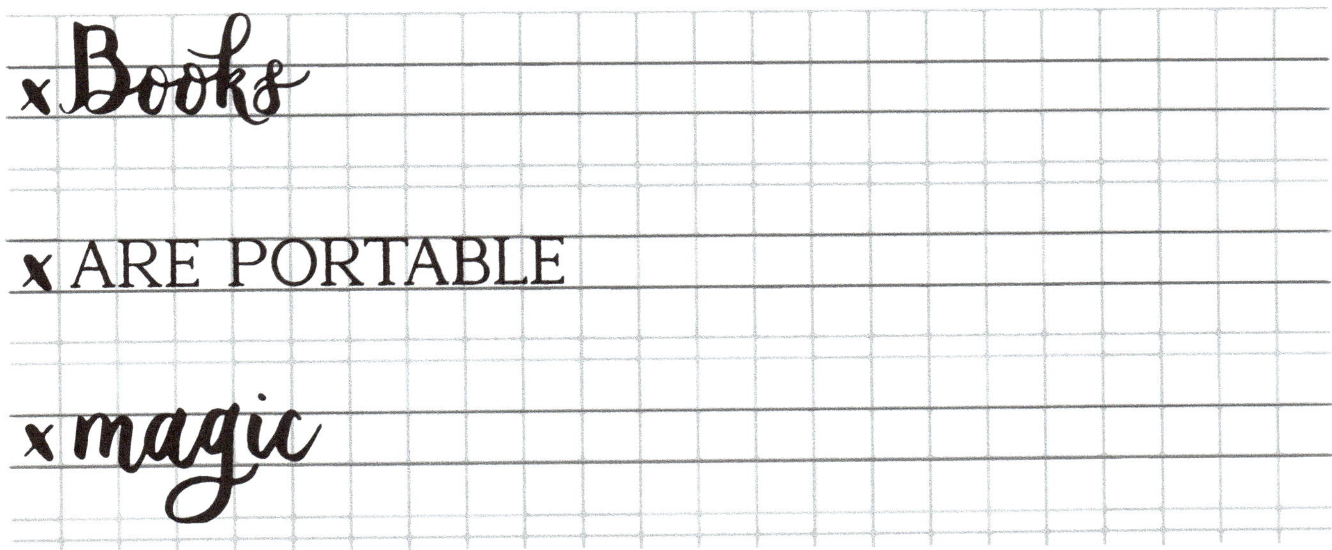

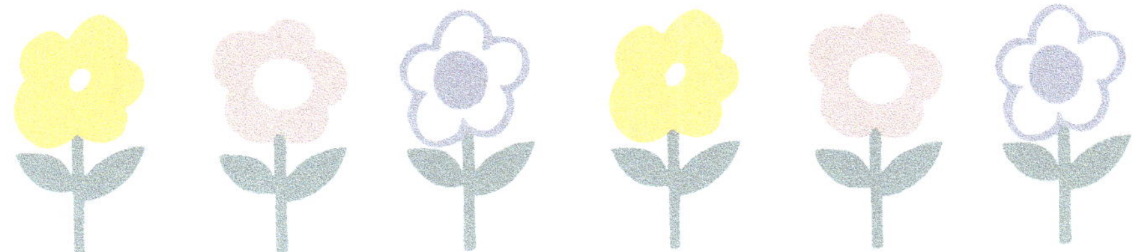

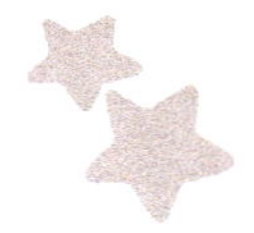

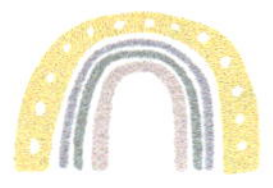

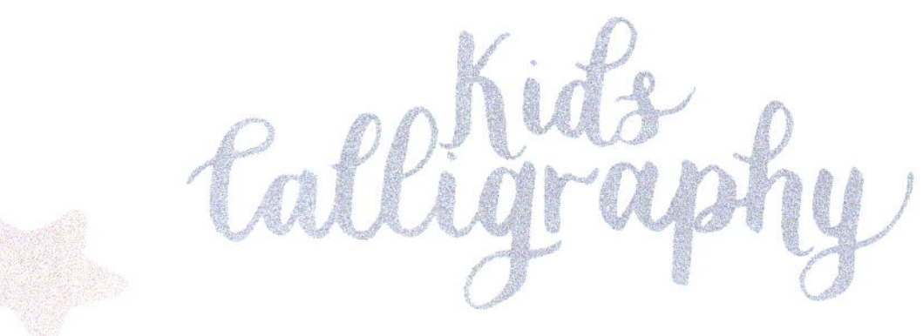

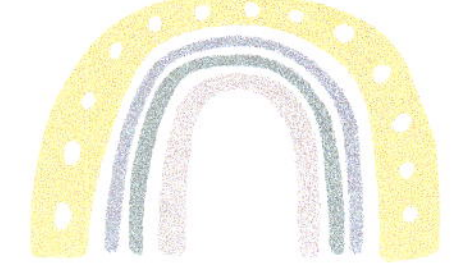

"BOOKS ARE PORTABLE MAGIC"

Use your brush pen calligraphy to create this special bookmark. What colour pens will you choose? You can decorate your bookmark with lots of fun pictures too. Or you can add glitter and stickers. You can punch a hole in the top and add a ribbon or tassle to decorate your bookmark. Get creative and enjoy yourself!

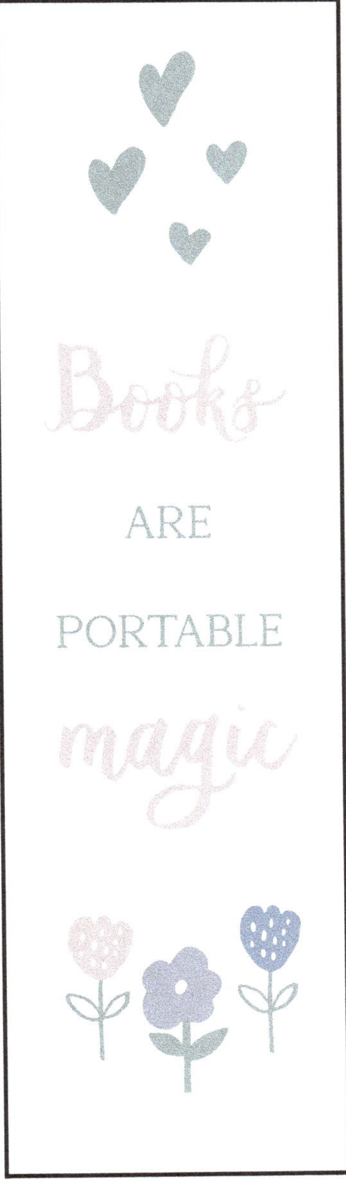

Kids Calligraphy

"JUST ONE MORE CHAPTER"

Practice the words below and then use the lay out of the book quotes on the next pages to create your own bookmark. You can choose any colours you like and decorate it with your own pictures! Remember to add a ribbon or tassle to your bookmark.

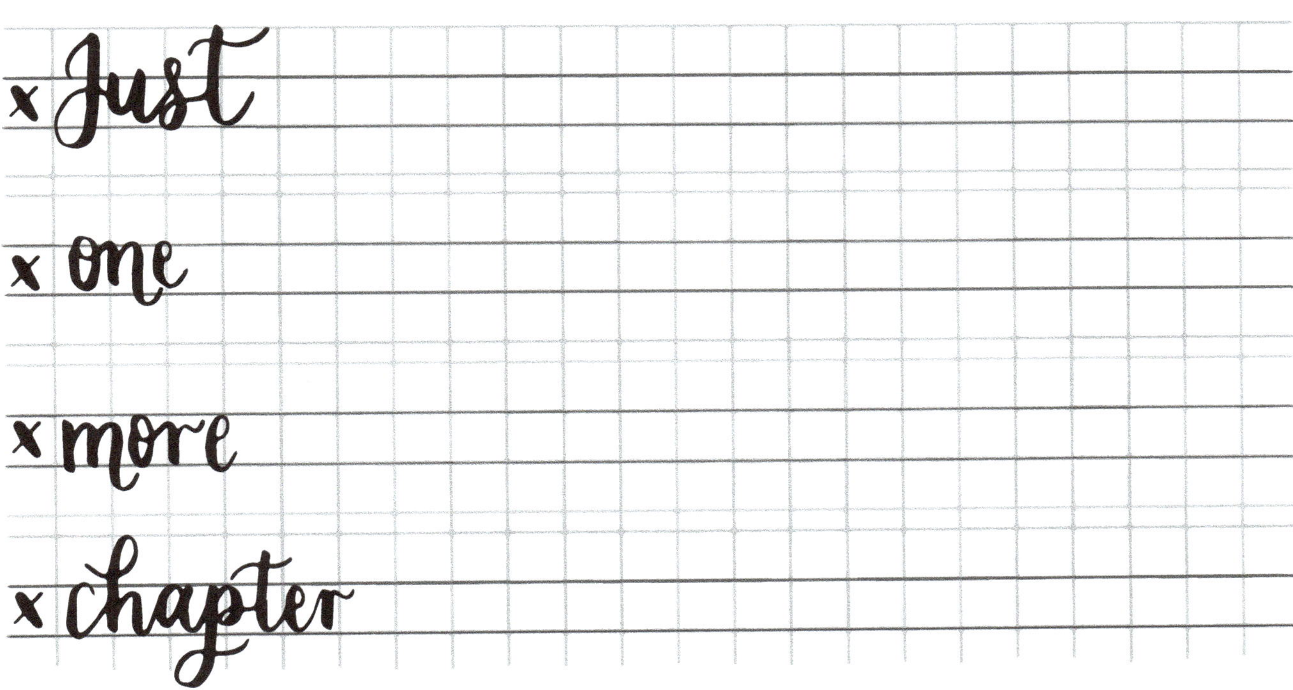

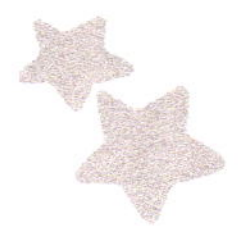
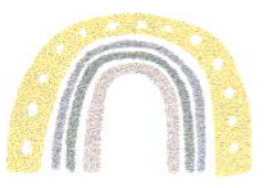

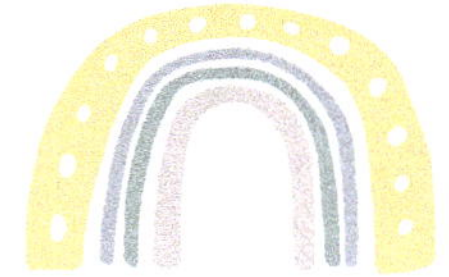

"JUST ONE MORE CHAPTER"

Use your brush pen calligraphy to create this special bookmark. What colour pens will you choose? You can decorate your bookmark with lots of fun pictures too. Or you can add glitter and stickers. You can punch a hole in the top and add a ribbon or tassle to decorate your bookmark. Get creative and enjoy yourself!

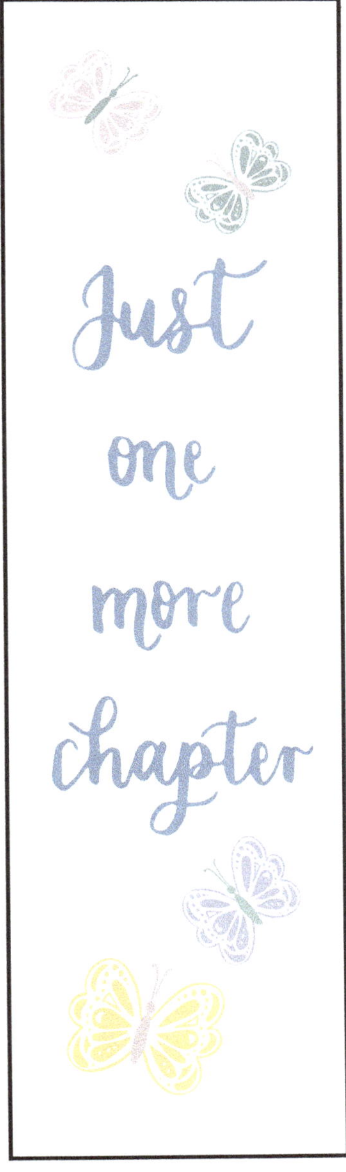

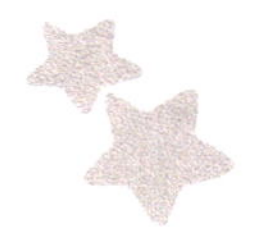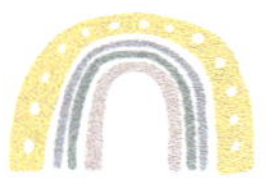

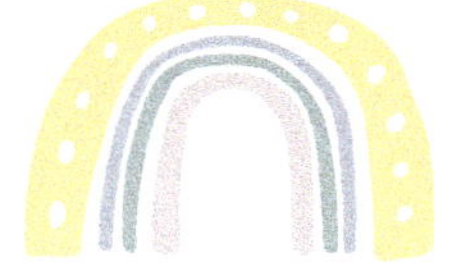

"READING IS DREAMING WITH OPEN EYES"

Practice the words below and then use the lay out of the book quotes on the next pages to create your own bookmark. You can choose any colours you like and decorate it with your own pictures! Remember to add a ribbon or tassle to your bookmark.

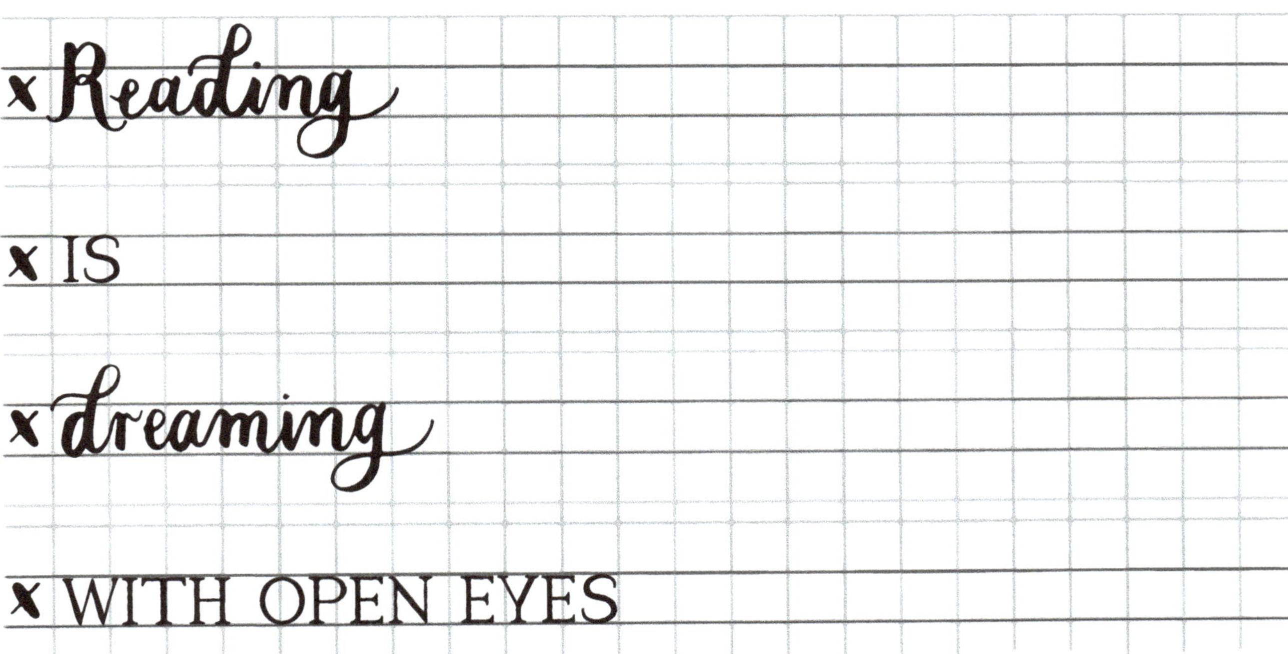

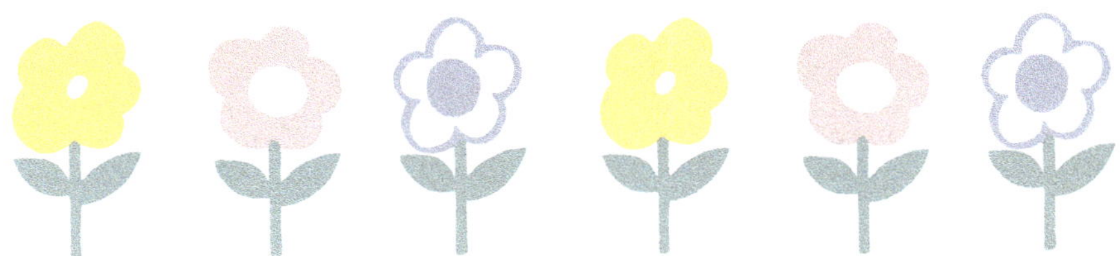

BOOKMARK EXAMPLE

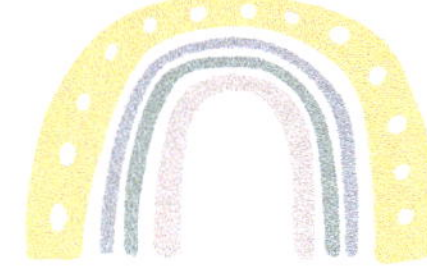

"READING IS DREAMING WITH OPEN EYES"

Use your brush pen calligraphy to create this special bookmark. What colour pens will you choose? You can decorate your bookmark with lots of fun pictures too. Or you can add glitter and stickers. You can punch a hole in the top and add a ribbon or tassle to decorate your bookmark. Get creative and enjoy yourself!

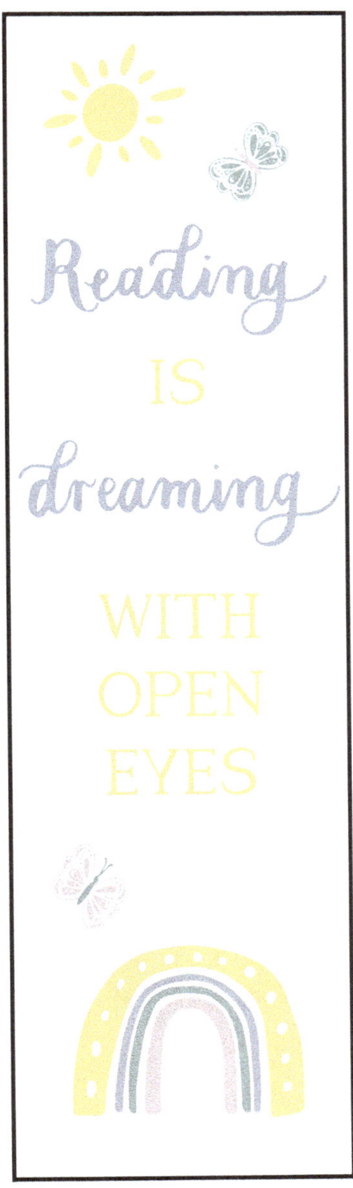

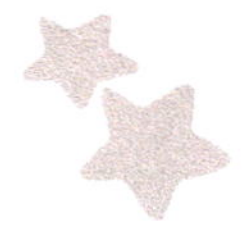
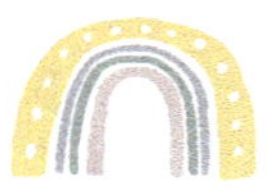

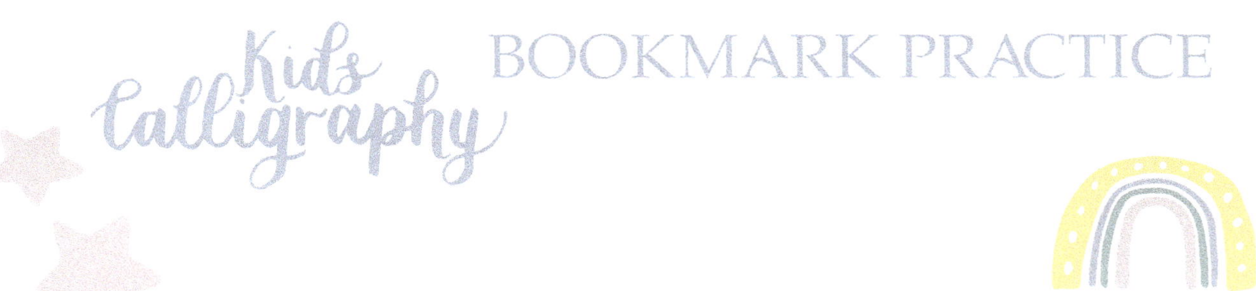

"SO MANY BOOKS, SO LITTLE TIME"

Practice the words below and then use the lay out of the book quotes on the next pages to create your own bookmark. You can choose any colours you like and decorate it with your own pictures! Remember to add a ribbon or tassle to your bookmark.

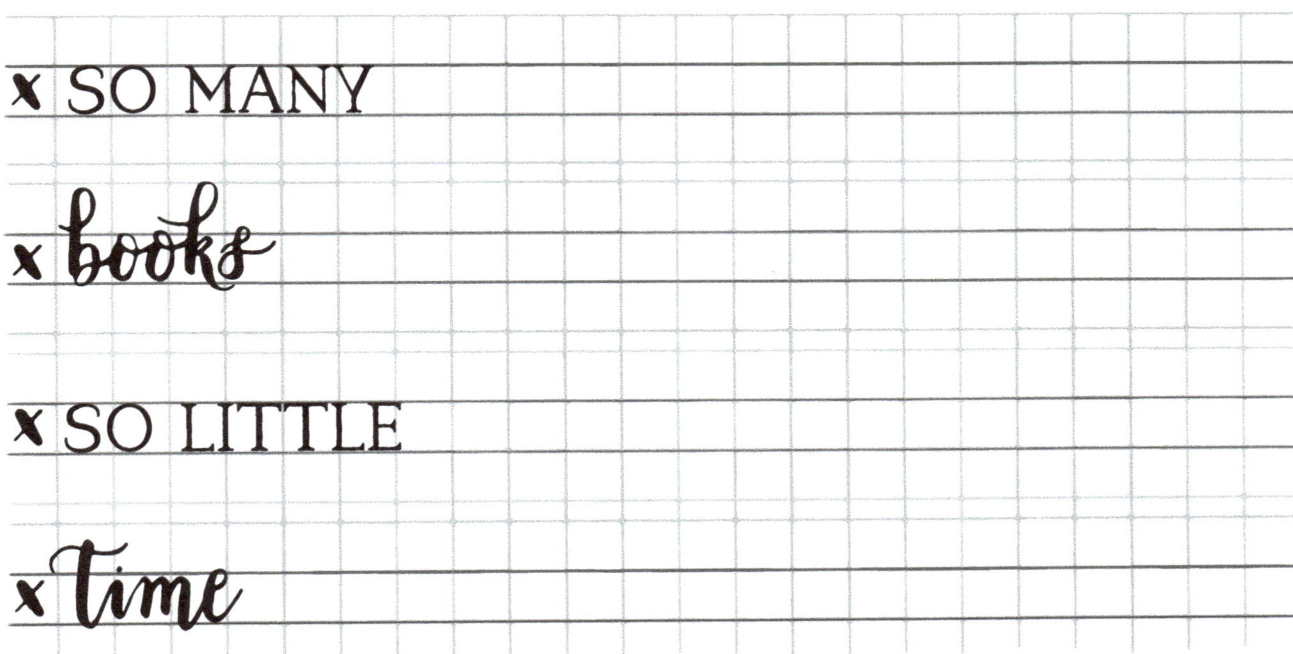

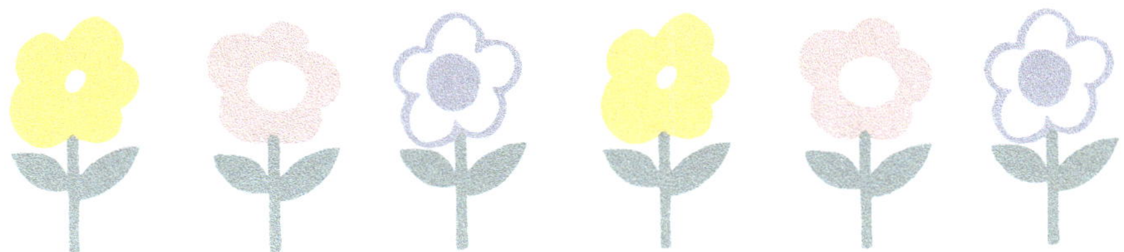

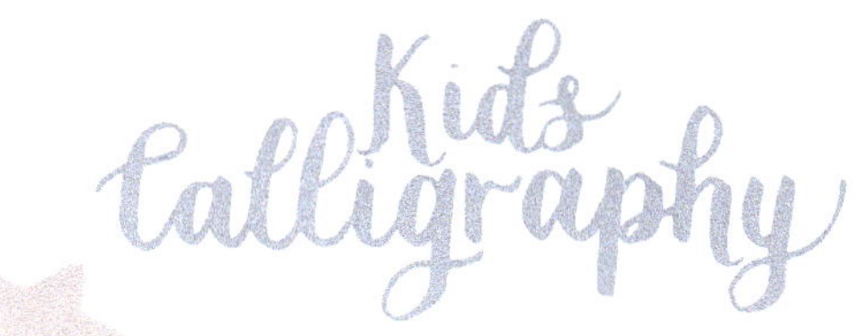 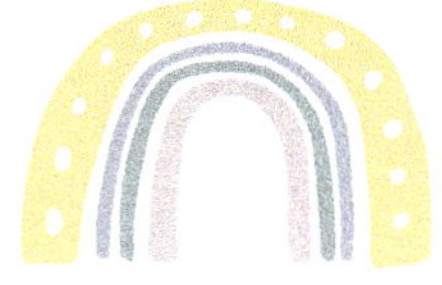

BOOKMARK EXAMPLE

"SO MANY BOOKS, SO LITTLE TIME"

Use your brush pen calligraphy to create this special bookmark. What colour pens will you choose? You can decorate your bookmark with lots of fun pictures too. Or you can add glitter and stickers. You can punch a hole in the top and add a ribbon or tassle to decorate your bookmark. Get creative and enjoy yourself!

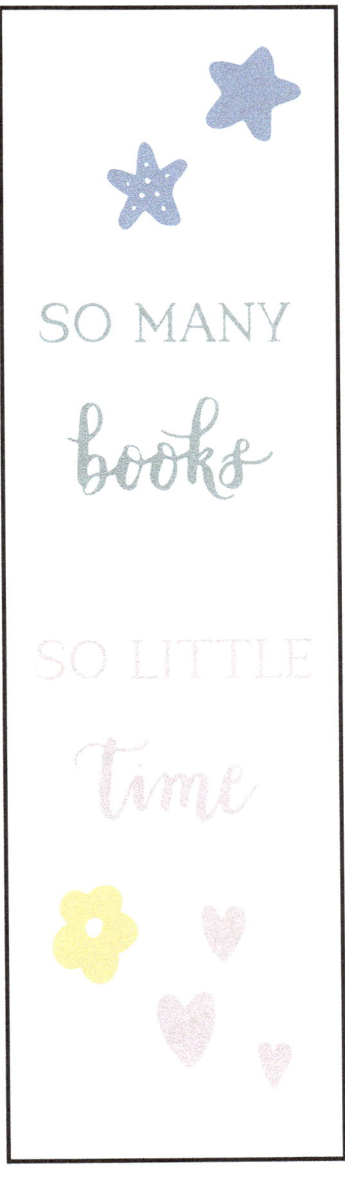

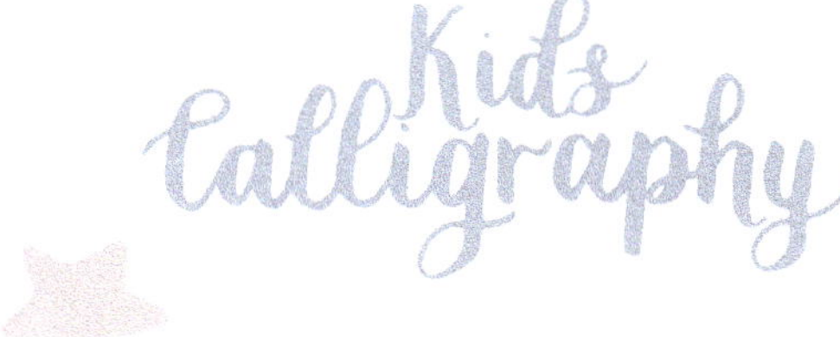

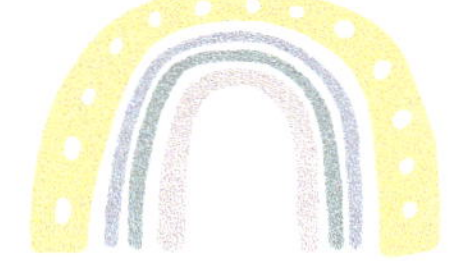

"YOU FELL ASLEEP HERE"

Practice the words below and then use the lay out of the book quotes on the next pages to create your own bookmark. You can choose any colours you like and decorate it with your own pictures! Remember to add a ribbon or tassle to your bookmark.

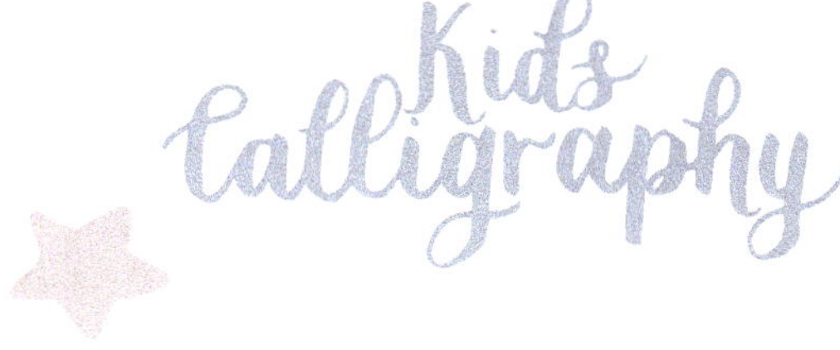

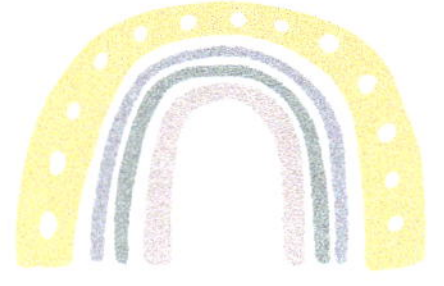

"YOU FELL ASLEEP HERE"

Use your brush pen calligraphy to create this special bookmark. What colour pens will you choose? You can decorate your bookmark with lots of fun pictures too. Or you can add glitter and stickers. You can punch a hole in the top and add a ribbon or tassle to decorate your bookmark. Get creative and enjoy yourself!

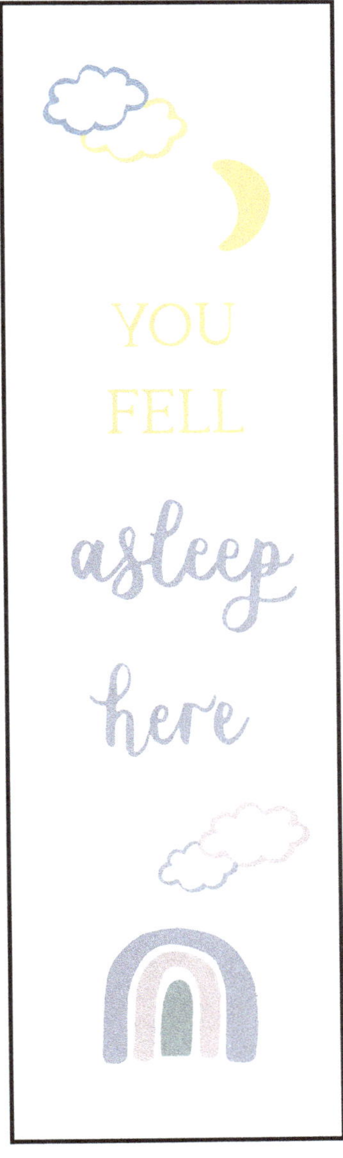

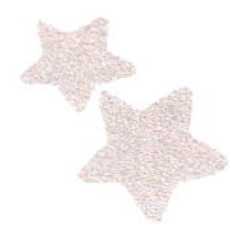
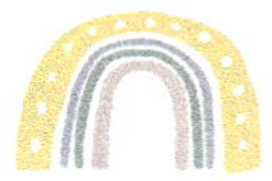

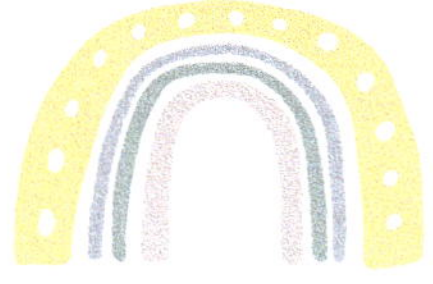

MAKING A BOOKMARK

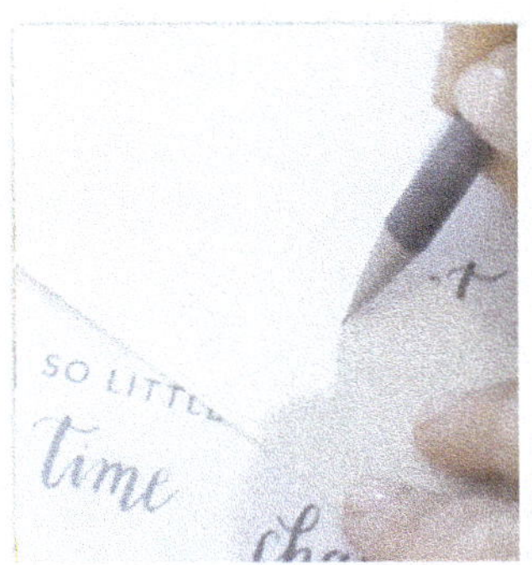

Ruling the lines and writing the letters in pencil

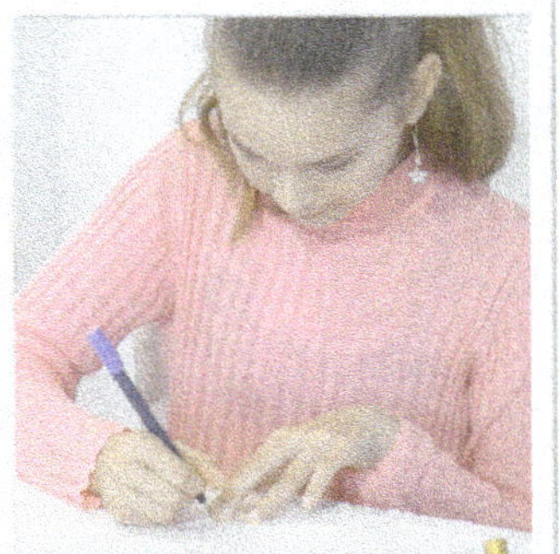

Practicing the brush pen calligraphy lettering

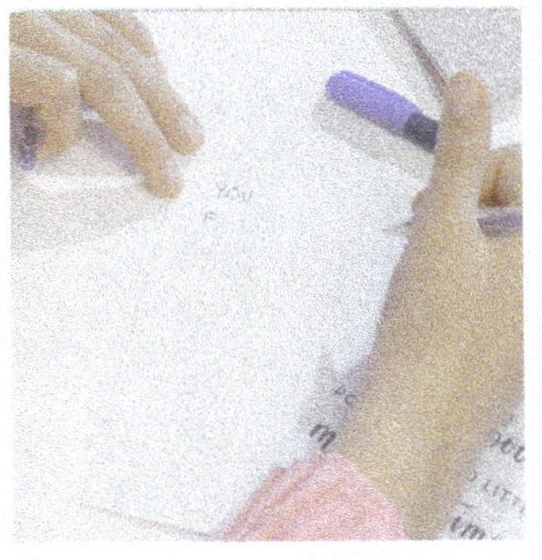

Writing the capital letters using a gel pen

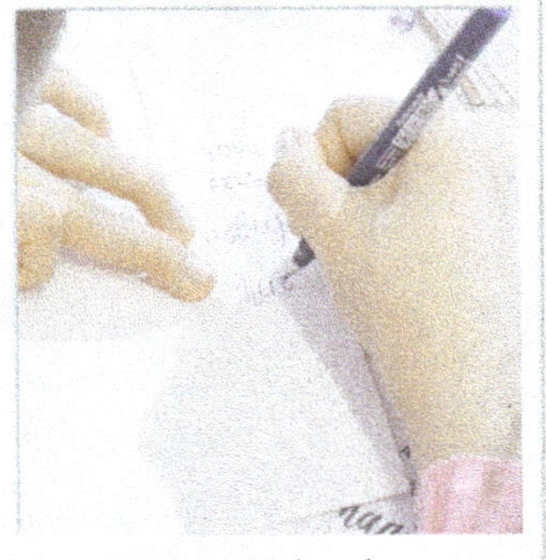

Writing the brush pen calligraphy

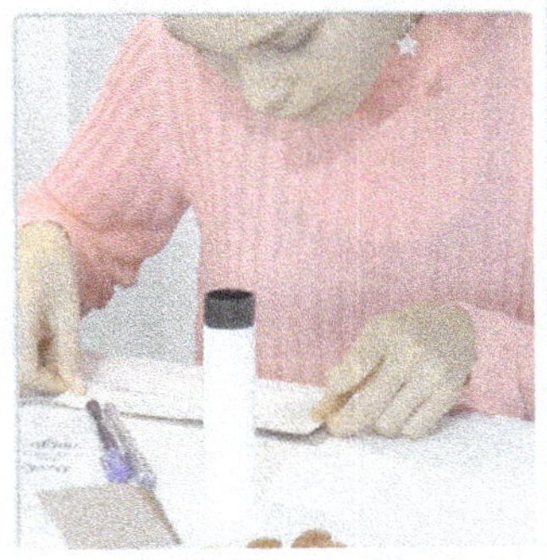

Gluing the bookmark onto a colourful card background

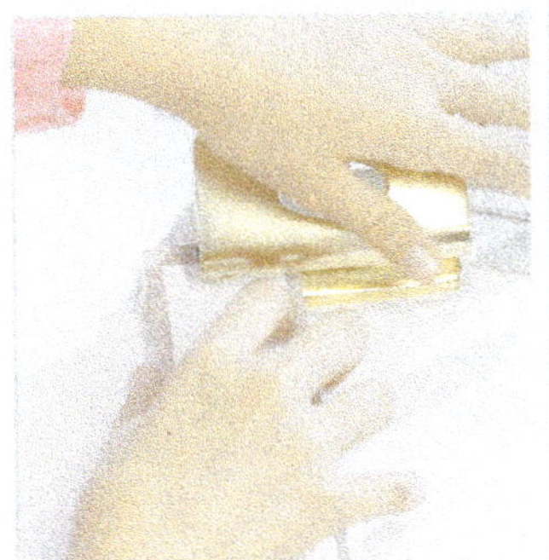

Punching a hole in the top of the bookmark

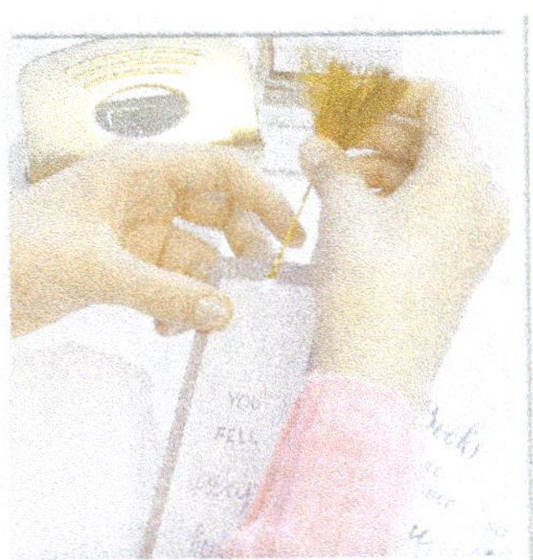

Putting a tassle through the hole and the bookmark's finished.

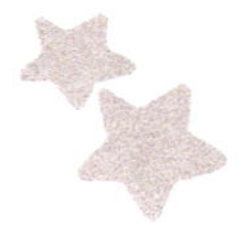

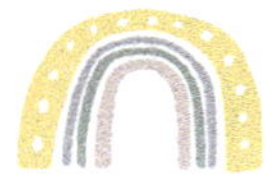

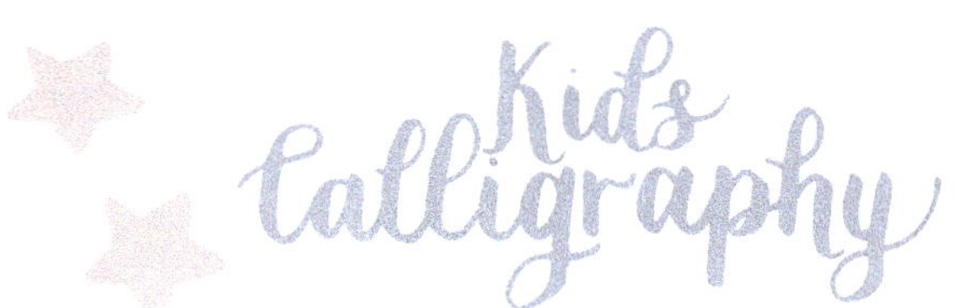 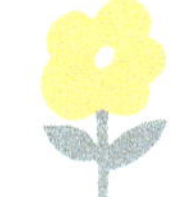 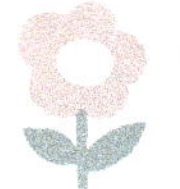 

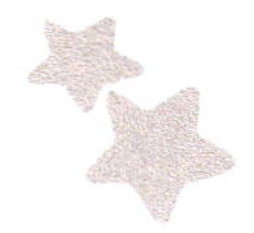
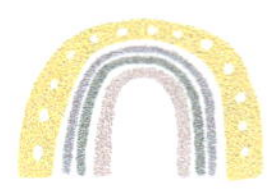

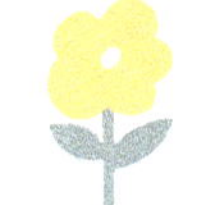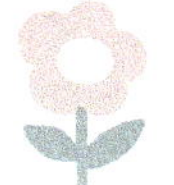

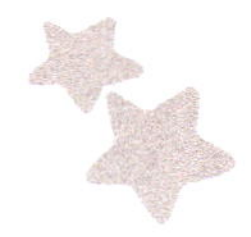 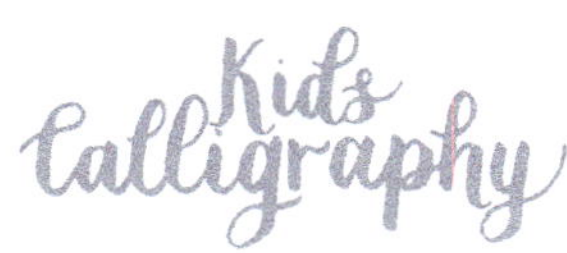 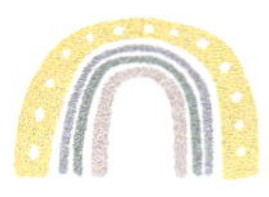

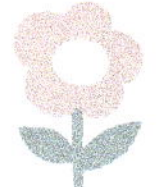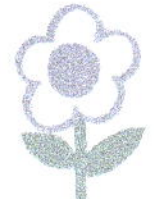

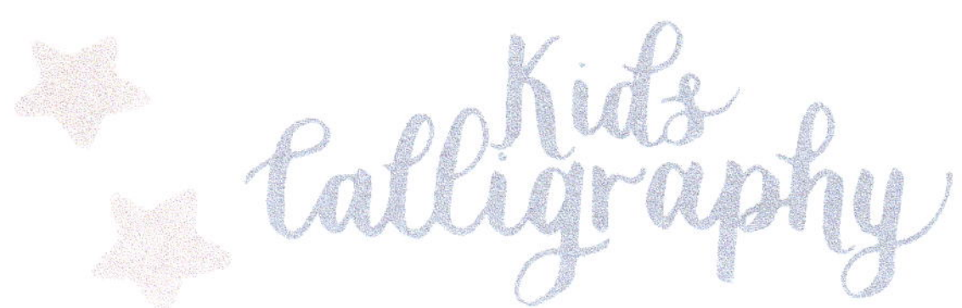 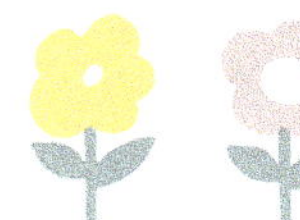 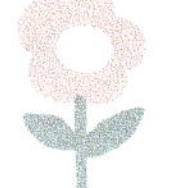 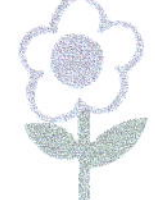

EXTRA PRACTICE SHEETS

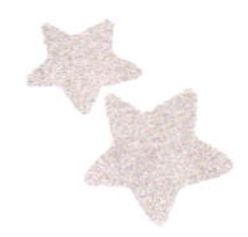

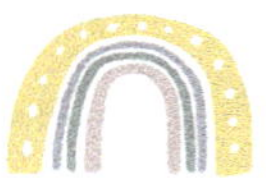

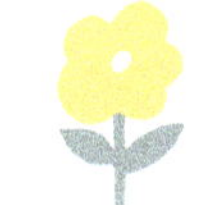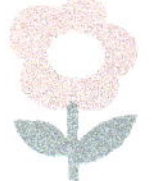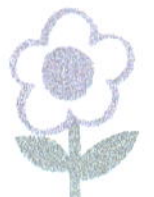

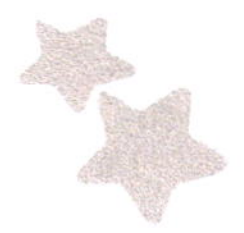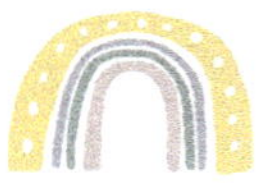

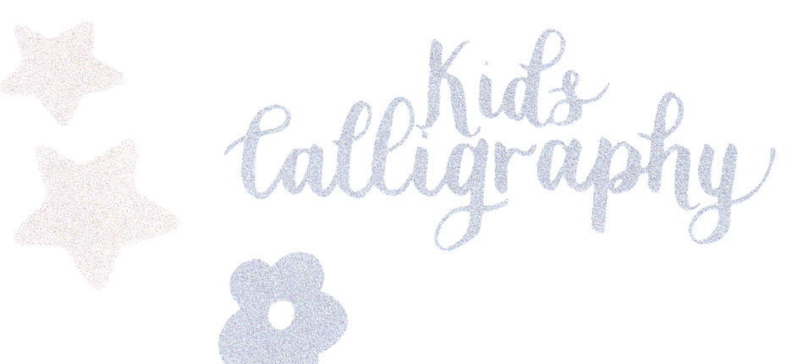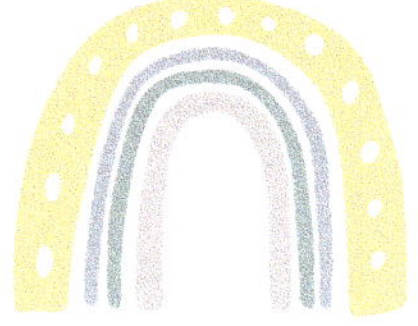

If you are reading this page, it means you have completed all the practice and training in the book.

WELL DONE!

I hope you have enjoyed the journey of learning brush pen calligraphy. I'm sure you enjoyed creating bookmarks, wall art, and greeting cards too. These are just some of the cool projects you can do with your calligraphy. You are really only limited by your imagination to create lots more beautiful pieces of art.

And this is really only the start of the journey. There are lots of different kinds of calligraphy that you can learn. Such as dip pen calligraphy or brush calligraphy. Keep exploring and keep practicing. And in no time you'll have beautiful handwriting.

Enjoy the process of learning and the journey of calligraphy!

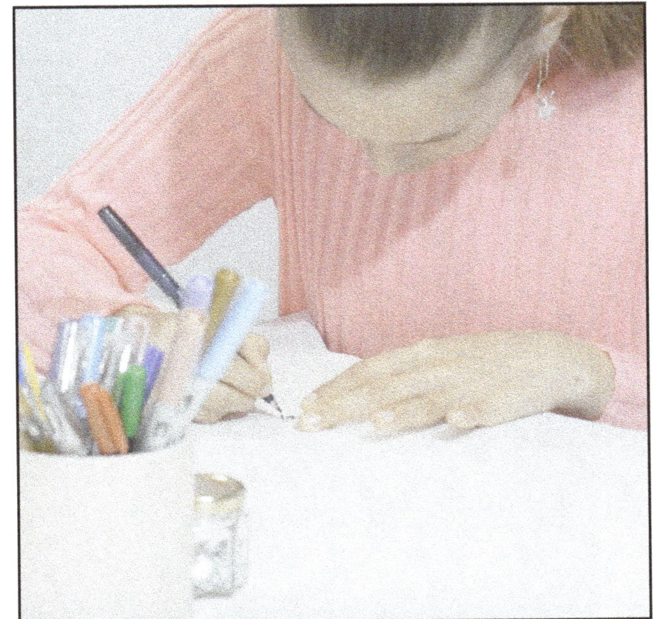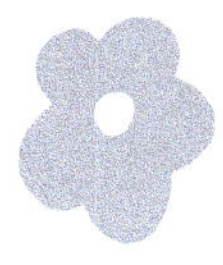

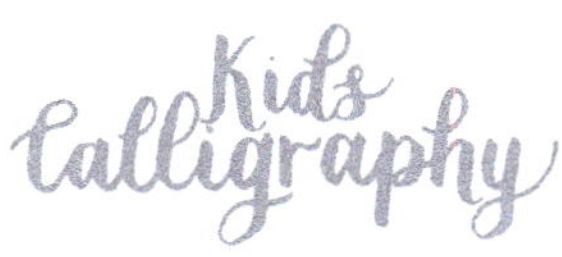
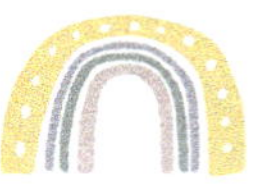

ABOUT THE AUTHOR

Emma is the calligrapher at Inkberry Calligraphy, an art studio based in stunning Auckland, New Zealand. She has been doing calligraphy for over 35 years. She creates bespoke calligraphy art pieces, stationery for weddings, lettering for events and luxury brands, and also teaches calligraphy in face to face lessons and workshops.

Emma is especially passionate about encouraging children's calligraphy skills. She knows that in a fast-paced technical world, a focus on hand-writing and creativity is ever more important for children's development. By promoting the skills of handwritten lettering, she is trying to preserve the beautiful, ancient art of calligraphy...one letter at a time!

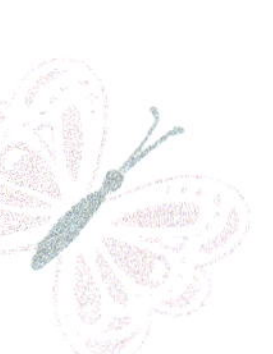
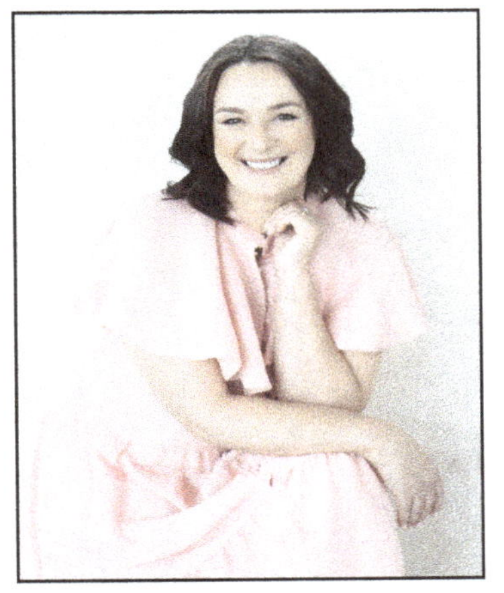

EMMA PEARCE-HAGEN
CALLIGRAPHER AT INKBERRY CALLIGRAPHY

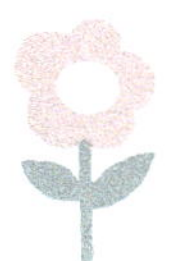

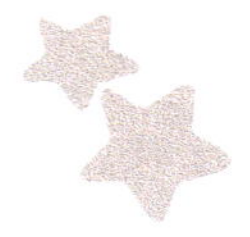
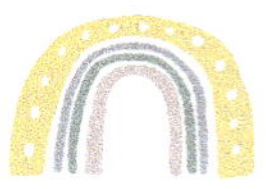